FRENCH BULLDOG

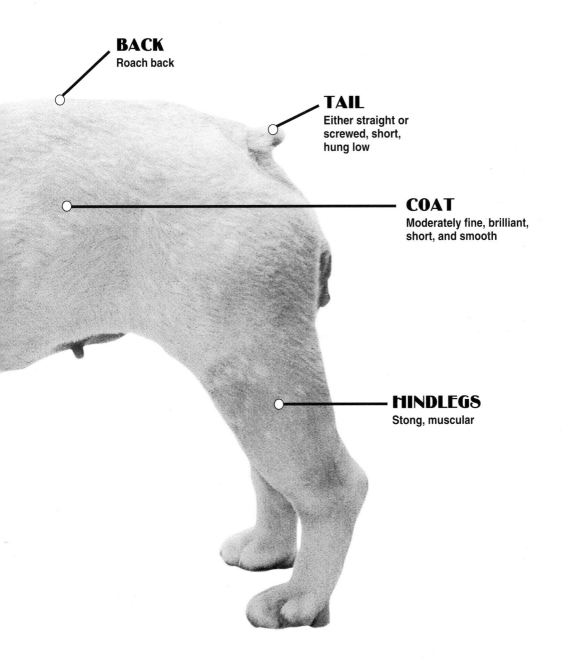

BACK
Roach back

TAIL
Either straight or
screwed, short,
hung low

COAT
Moderately fine, brilliant,
short, and smooth

HINDLEGS
Stong, muscular

Title Page: Ch. Lefox Cherie Clair de Lune owned by Doris and Henry Bohunek.

Photographers: Sandra Goose Allen, Kathy Dannel, Downey Dog Show Photography, Isabelle Francais, Muriel Lee, Pets by Paulette, Colette Secher.

© T.F.H. Publications, Inc.

Distributed in the UNITED STATES to the Pet Trade by T.F.H. Publications, Inc., 1 TFH Plaza, Neptune City, NJ 07753; on the Internet at www.tfh.com; in CANADA by Rolf C. Hagen Inc., 3225 Sartelon St., Montreal, Quebec H4R 1E8; Pet Trade by H & L Pet Supplies Inc., 27 Kingston Crescent, Kitchener, Ontario N2B 2T6; in ENGLAND by T.F.H. Publications, PO Box 74, Havant PO9 5TT; in AUSTRALIA AND THE SOUTH PACIFIC by T.F.H. (Australia), Pty. Ltd., Box 149, Brookvale 2100 N.S.W., Australia; in NEW ZEALAND by Brooklands Aquarium Ltd., 5 McGiven Drive, New Plymouth, RD1 New Zealand; in SOUTH AFRICA by Rolf C. Hagen S.A. (PTY.) LTD., P.O. Box 201199, Durban North 4016, South Africa; in JAPAN by T.F.H. Publications. Published by T.F.H. Publications, Inc.

MANUFACTURED IN THE
UNITED STATES OF AMERICA
BY T.F.H. PUBLICATIONS, INC.

FRENCH BULLDOG

A COMPLETE AND RELIABLE HANDBOOK

Muriel Lee

RX-145

CONTENTS

INTRODUCTION TO THE FRENCH BULLDOG

The French Bulldog! It is not a well-known or popular breed, but what a star in the canine universe! No, the French Bulldog is not a small Bulldog nor a large Boston Terrier, but is a unique breed that has the most endearing personality and manner that you will find among any breed.

This book will give you an overview of the breed, its history, its description, and the standard. You will also learn about puppy care, training, and the health of the breed. With wonderful color photographs you will see that the French Bulldog is as handsome as they come, and that his wit and clownish ways will be hard to beat.

This may not be the dog for everyone. He is not an extremely active dog that will work a field or go on a long hike with you. He is a French "gentleman" who

Although the French Bulldog is not one of the most popular breeds of dog, his lovable personality and good nature make him a desirable pet.

likes the finer things in life and whose primary purpose is to keep his master happy. However, if this is what you are looking for, then the Frenchie may be just the dog for you. And as is true with most breeds, once you give your heart and home to a French Bulldog, you will remain a devotee to the breed for a lifetime.

It is written, "Tis better to have loved and lost a Frenchie than never to have loved at all."

The Frenchie aims to please! By nature, the French Bulldog is not an athletic or extremely active dog. However, he will go to great lengths to please his master.

HISTORY OF THE FRENCH BULLDOG

In the history of the dog world, the French Bulldog is not an ancient breed; however, its beginnings can be traced back as early as the 1850s, and it is one of the older breeds accepted by the American Kennel Club (AKC).

In 1884, the American Kennel Club was formed for the purpose of setting up a uniform set of rules so that anyone competing in a dog show anywhere in the country would be competing under the same conditions. All breeds of dog were placed into two divisions—the Sporting dogs, which included all breeds that were bred to work, and the Non-Sporting dogs,

The French Bulldog's origin can be traced to the 1850s. Many historians believe that the unique breed's roots go back to the English Bulldog.

GROUP
FIRST
MINNEAPOLIS
KENNEL CLUB
NOVEMBER
1997
PHOTO BY DOWNEY

Non-Sporting Group

which included all other breeds. With the passing of time, the Sporting Group was broken down into the Sporting, Hound, and Terrier, and the Toy breeds were classified into a group of their own. Eventually, the Working Group was formed and in more recent years, the Herding or pastoral dogs were taken from the Working Group and given their own classification. The French Bulldog began in and has remained in the Non-Sporting Group or Utility Group in the UK. Today, there are seven classifications in the AKC: Sporting, Hound, Working, Terrier, Toy, Non-Sporting, and Herding.

The French Bulldog is part of the Non-Sporting Group and is one of the older breeds accepted by the American Kennel Club. One of the top-winning Frenchies of all time, Ch. Lefox Goodtime Steel Magnolia, handled by Jane Flowers.

At the present time, the Non-Sporting Group includes 16 breeds: the American Eskimo Dog, Bichon Frise, Boston Terrier, Bulldog, Chinese Shar-Pei, Chow Chow, Dalmatian, Finnish Spitz, French Bulldog, Keeshond, Lhasa Apso, Poodle, Schipperke, Shiba Inu, Tibetan Spaniel, and Tibetan Terrier. As can be seen, the French Bulldog is in the company of a most diverse group of dogs. They vary in body type, conformation, and coat, as well as in personality and the purpose for which each dog was bred.

In his native territory, the French Bulldog was known as the Bouledogue Francais and fortunately his origins can be traced a bit easier than the origins of some other breeds. Most historians believe that the French Bulldog's roots go back to the English Bulldog, a very old breed that traces its ancestry back to the ancient Mastiff.

Bulldogs were used for bullbaiting in the Middle Ages in England. To have an understanding of Bulldog history, it is helpful to have some knowledge of the British Isles during the 1700s and early 1800s. Times were hard, the general populace was poor, and cruelty to animals was as common as cruelty to one another. Dogfighting, with its prior background of badger-, bear-, and bullbaiting, was not outlawed in England until 1835. Until then, dogfighting (and previously bullbaiting) was one of the more popular sports for the common people. At that time, little or no concern was given to the cruelty of the sport. Living

Although their ancestors were used in the sport of bullbaiting, Frenchies were also known for their loyalty and affection for their masters.

conditions were tough and, by and large, people were uneducated. Dogfighting provided an entertainment that was cheap and exciting, and in addition offered the spectators an opportunity to place their bets on the side. Picture the dogs opposing one another in a pit similar to a boxing ring, with the raucous spectators pressed up against the walls, urging their favorite animal to get the better of his opponent. Amid the clamor and noise (and smells, as one can imagine), money was passing through hands as the dogs were ready to fight to the death of their opponent. It was not a pretty picture.

By the time bullbaiting was outlawed, the Bulldog was a common breed in English life and he was considered to be a symbol of courage, stamina, and bravery by the English populace.

The breeders of the Bulldog began to diversify. One group crossbred with Terriers for speed and agility, and these dogs eventually evolved into the Bull Terrier and the Staffordshire Bull Terrier. Another group started to breed a smaller Bulldog that weighed between 16 and 25 pounds. This was a rather ragtag group of dogs, with some dogs having rose or erect ears, some with bodies that were short and high on leg, and some with flat faces and long muzzles. These dogs did not appeal to the majority of Bulldog breeders; however, the small breed did have its supporters, particularly with the English working class. As the Industrial Revolution grew in England and the workers were replaced by machines, many artisans (especially the lace makers) from the Midlands—Nottingham, Birmingham, and Sheffield—moved to France and took their small Bulldogs with them. Because the Bulldog breeders were not fond of these small dogs, they were happy to see them move on to France and continued to send the small dogs to the continent.

Between 1860 and 1900, the Bouledogue Francais became very popular in France, particularly among the prostitutes, or "belles de nuit," in Paris. They were seen along the boulevards and in the cafes with the fancy ladies, and the famous artist, Toulouse-Lautrec, placed them in his wonderful paintings and drawings of Parisian nightlife.

By 1890, the Frenchie was being sent back to England. During that time, Mr. George Krehl became a leading importer of the breed to the English shores. Worried that the English would change their little

French import, the French wrote up a standard for the breed, which is fairly close to the present-day French Bulldog standard. The French, although lax in their record keeping, were determined to keep the Frenchie a compact, straight-legged, short-faced dog. They did not want to copy the exaggerated features of the English Bulldog.

In the meantime, the small group of breeders in England who had never abandoned their Toy Bulldog found that interest in their breed was waning as the public's awareness of the attractive newcomer from France increased. By 1920, the Toy Bulldog had become another breed that disappeared into the canine history books, where it has since remained.

French Bulldogs were imported to the United States early on, and by the late 1800s, the breed had attracted a dedicated and enthusiastic group of American fanciers who were producing Frenchies that were consistent in type and size.

The breed was first exhibited in America in 1896 at the Westminster Kennel Club show before it received recognition from the AKC. Newspaper coverage of

Determined to keep the French Bulldog a compact, straight-legged, short-faced dog, the French wrote an official standard for the breed.

In the early 1900s, the French Bulldog made the move from England and was one of the most popular breeds in America. His Majesty King Edward VII is pictured here with his French Bulldog companion.

this event was enthusiastic because the dogs were owned by prominent women from American society. By the following year, the entries at Westminster had doubled. The judge, an English gentleman, selected dogs with rose ears for first-place wins, as they were proper on the Bulldog. Following the judging, the Americans, dismayed that the Frenchie bat ear had not been acknowledged, held a meeting and immediately formed the French Bulldog Club of America (FBDCA). They drafted the US standard for the breed, whereby bat ears were accepted as the proper ear for the French Bulldog.

The first AKC-sanctioned breed show was held in 1898 at the Waldorf-Astoria Hotel in New York City.

The show was greeted with great interest and enthusiasm by the press as this was the first sanctioned show of the breed and the first time a specialty show of any breed had been held in such lavish surroundings. In addition, New York society was in attendance. The *New York Herald* reported, "Never was a bench show held within so sumptuous an environment as that of the French Bulldog held at the Waldorf-Astoria yesterday afternoon and evening. Far up in the sun parlor, on the top most floor of the building, amid palms and potted plants and rich rugs and soft divans, 50 bulldogs were on exhibition."

The Frenchie was a favorite with East Coast society and a number of prominent names were associated with the breed. Frenchies gained rapidly in popularity, and at the 1903 Westminster show there was an entry of 82 dogs. By 1906, the entry was an even 100. At that time, the French Bulldog was the fifth most popular breed in America.

In 1905, Samuel Goldenberg entered Westminster with the French import, Nellcote Gamin. He was a small (under 22 pounds) brindle dog that was considered to be the most perfect representation of the breed up to that time. He was an outstanding show dog, but his lasting mark on the breed was as a superior stud dog. Gamin, if one had a pedigree form large enough, would be in the background of most of today's champion dogs. At the time, it was written that "no dog who ever lived has done so much for the breed."

By 1907, it was recognized both in Europe and England that the Americans had the best French Bulldogs and that they had perfected the breed's unique bat ear. Forever after, the bat ear was the acceptable ear for the breed worldwide.

Eventually, Ch. Nellcote Gamin was sold to Fred and Warren Purdy, brothers who had been breeding Frenchies since 1904. Gamin lived a long and productive life with the Purdys, producing exceptional champions, one of which was Ch. Pourquoi Pas, the foundation dog of the famous Never-Never-Land Kennels, owned by the Broadway actress, Mary Winthrop Turner.

Mrs. Turner, although only active in the breed for a short five years, worked with excellent kennel managers who assisted her in buying and breeding excellent Frenchies. Ch. Parsque was considered to have the best head and ear carriage of any Frenchie prior to that time and was also a prepotent sire. At the specialty in 1914, 14 of his 15 were entered first in their classes.

In the Midwest, the Normandy Kennels were founded by Dr. and Mrs. F. A. Fisher. They owned another Gamin son, Ch. Gamin de Luxe, whom Dr. Fisher considered to be the best example of the breed in his kennel. The Fishers had a large kennel and sold puppies throughout the Central and Western states. They were the first two breeder-judges of the French Bulldog and were well-known throughout the US.

By 1913, 142 Frenchies were entered at the French Bulldog Club of New England specialty. This was to be the high point of popularity for the breed; several decades later the breed started to decline.

A number of breeders, primarily Frederic Poffet and John Maginnis, worked actively as guardians of the breed during this declining period. Mr. Poffet, a Frenchman who moved to New York in 1895, was very active in the breed from 1901 until his death at the age of 94 (the last time he exhibited a dog was at the age of 89). In addition to breeding and exhibiting under the kennel prefix, LaFrance, he was also the president of the FBDCA. Mr. Maginnis owned Ch. Miss Modesty, whelped in 1935, who won the Non-Sporting Group 69 times and was all-breed Best in Show 4 times.

Mr. and Mrs. George Jeffrey from Short Hills, New Jersey, were active in the breed in the late 1940s and 1950s. Ch. Le Petit Marquis de la France II, whelped in 1946, won Best of Breed four times at the prestigious Morris and Essex show and won the French Bulldog Club of America specialty in 1949, 1950, and 1951, retiring the club's challenge trophy.

Ralph and Amanda West of Ralanda Kennels in Livonia, Michigan, were prominent in the breed in the 1950s and 1960s. They loved cream-colored Frenchies and are responsible for the present-day creams. They owned Am./Can. Ch. Bouquet Nouvelle Ami, bred by Bernard Strauss, who won 37 all-breed Bests in Show between 1956 and 1958. In addition, he was Best of Breed at Westminster for eight consecutive years and the National Specialty winner for four consecutive years. Ch. Berneil's Jeepers Jackie, bred by Neil McAllister and owned by the Wests, won four Bests in Show and was a top Non-Sporting dog in 1959 and 1960. Ch. Ralanda Ami Francine won 55 all-breed Bests in Show between 1961 and 1964 and won the

Ken-L Ration award in 1962 and 1964. The Wests felt that Francine was the best Frenchie that they had ever owned.

A well-known breeder in the 1970s was Mrs. Lavender Lovell of Connecticut. Her Ch. Chaseholm Mr. Chips was a top East Coast winner, and this brindle dog and his colorful owner were known by many.

The lean years for the French Bulldog were in the 1950s and 1960s. During this period, the average registration per year was less than 100, and one year entries at the national specialty show fell to a low point of 15.

In the 1950s and 1960s, the majority of French Bulldogs that were being bred were on the West Coast. Lucretia Bedal and Enid Ramos worked together and with their breeding programs cooperatively produced some fine dogs. However, their mark on the breed was to place puppies with Janis Hampton and Dick and Angel Terrette.

Because of their silly antics and friendly disposition, Frenchies make wonderful companions for both children and adults.

The Terrettes bought their first show Frenchie from Mrs. Bedal, bred their first litter, and continued to breed until Dick's death in 1981. Not only did they breed some wonderful Frenchies, but Dick put obedience titles on many of them. The couple worked

together on their breeding program and bred animals that complimented one another, in addition to having good pedigrees and good backgrounds. Their foundation bitch, purchased in 1936, was Terrette's Mitzi, CD. Mitzi's first litter produced the dog that was to become their foundation dog, Ch. Terrette's Chef D'Oeuvres, CDX (Ricki). Their kennel produced many great dogs, some that they kept and showed and other dogs that were sold and shown by their new owners. They exported several Frenchies to England and to Europe. Ch. Terrette's Bourbillon D'Gamin, CD, a Ricki grandson, sired 35 champions. In addition to the dogs, they also produced superb bitches that were a credit to the breed.

Mrs. Hampton became active in the breed in the late 1940s. Her foundation bitch, Ch. Bedal's Menjou LeChef D'Oeuvre, was obtained from Mrs. Bedal. Mrs. Hampton has put championships on over 30 Frenchies. The first time she showed Menjou, she met the Terretts. Her dogs have won from coast to coast and she has judged throughout the world. Having an excellent eye for the breed, she has been a formidable guardian of the French Bulldog, encouraging every Frenchie breeder to breed the best dogs possible, to know and follow the standard, and to remember that the French Bulldog is bred as a companion dog—one who will respond to your every mood.

The Terretts and Janis Hampton became lifelong friends, and Dick was the individual who gave Janis the encouragement to get out in the ring and show her dogs. Mrs. Hampton is not only a famous breeder but also a well-known judge of all Non-Sporting dogs. She has since retired from her judging duties. Janis and the Terretts worked cooperatively on their breeding programs and between them produced over 70 champions. She wrote, "My involvement with the Terretts all the years has given me the best in friendship, advice and propagation of lovely dogs."

The Nordfelts of Laurelwood Kennels bred many champions. Their Ch. Laurelwood Jeep sired 19 champions. They also had a team of Frenchies that were Best in Show at the Los Angeles Kennel Club show.

The Frenchie's popularity has rebounded in recent decades and is now around 80th in popularity on the AKC's registration list. There are many breeders currently making an impact on the breed in the United States.

James Bigham and Bud Niles of Balihai Kennels have bred some 30 champions and have imported Frenchies from several European countries. Herschel and Doris Cox of Goodtime Kennels have produced over 40 champions, including Ch. Cox's Goodtime Ace in the Hole, one of the all-time top producing stud dogs in the Non-Sporting Group. In 1987, he sired 14 champions. Ch. Goodtime Charley Brown, sired by Ace in the Hole, had sired 83 champions in his lifetime.

Colette Secher's Kennel Lefox has produced many champions and Best in Show winners, most notably Ch. Lefox Goodtime Steel Magnolia, sired by Charley Brown and owned by Sally Sweatt. Magnolia won the breed at Westminster Kennel Club in 1992, 1994, and 1998, won six all-breed Bests in Show, and was Best of Opposite Sex at the FBDCA centenary show at the age of eight from the Veteran class.

Arlie Toye of LeBull Kennels has had winning Frenchies in addition to publishing an award-winning magazine, "The French Bullytin." Arlie has sponsored an evening each year at the National Specialty at which a French Bulldog fashion show has reigned as one of the high points of the Frenchie weekend.

Patricia and Luis Sosa of Bandog Kennels bred Ch. Bandog's Earnin' Respect, Number One Frenchie in 1990 and 1992. In addition, he won 11 all-breed Bests in Show and won the National Specialty three times, the last time from the Veteran class. Their Ch. Bandog's One in a Million was Number One Frenchie and Number Seven Non-Sporting dog in 1994. He was the 1993 National Specialty Winner and has 3 all-breed Bests in Show and over 30 group placements to his credit.

Other breeders to be mentioned are Robin Millican and Jayne Palmer of Kobi, Dr. Dorit Fisher of Belboulecan, Carol Taylor of Bullmarket Kennels, and Luca Carbone of Jaguar Kennels in California.

Time can only tell who the breeders of the future will be and who will have an impact on the breed to the extent that Janis Hampton, the Terretts, and the Coxs have had. The breed is in good condition and through the effort and dedication of the breeders of the future, it will remain so.

CHARACTERISTICS OF THE FRENCH BULLDOG

The French Bulldog is a no-nonsense companion dog. He may bark at a knock on the door and he may (or may not) chase a bunny that crosses his garden path, but he knows deep in his heart that God and the French (with an assist from the English and the Americans) have put him on earth to be a companion. He does not expect to do, nor will he do, a day's work, as would the Terrier, the Hound, or the Sporting dog. However, as a true companion, he is always ready for a bit of fun!

The Frenchie has the reputation of being a clown; a true comedian at heart. However, he can be quite dignified when it suits him, and he is also a faithful and devoted companion.

It's no surprise that these Frenchies are comfortable in their costumes. They are known to play dress-up and will easily tolerate whatever manner of dress their owner chooses.

National Geographic's *The Book of Dogs* noted, "He is a blithe spirit and beckons one to play at every glance. Diminutive, short-coated, sweet-tempered, and frisky. He was bred for genial companionship." Will Judy wrote an even better description in his 1936 *Dog Encyclopedia* (along with a photograph of a Frenchie sitting at a table, wearing a nice white shirt, while contemplating blowing out the candles on a birthday cake in front of him): "One must learn to like the Frenchie just as he learns to like olives, but once having learned to like the Frenchie, he will never cease to speak the praises of the breed. Not only in name but in mannerisms, the breed is French...He may look serious but he is a laughing philosopher, laughing not only with his mouth and eyes but with his entire body. He is always a clown, always ready for tricks but when he is at ease, he is the soul of dignity." And John Lynn Leonard wrote in 1928, "Once to possess one of this breed is always to love and admire him."

The French Bulldog is considered to be the clown of the canine breeds. Although the Sealyham Terrier will tolerate wearing caps and having cakes and candles for their birthday parties, the Frenchie actually likes to wear whatever manner of dress that is put on him. He likes caps, hats, and Mickey Mouse ears, and he is well-known for the Badger collars that he has worn since the late 1800s. He particularly likes sunglasses. At the Centennial Show held in Kansas City in 1998, the fashion contest found Frenchies dressed as Barbie dolls, bikini vamps, Turkish dancers, jesters, Uncle Sam, and Honey Bees and the Bee Keepers. A hit of the show was the Frenchie quartet dressed as the Idaho Potato family, complete with tater tots. Frenchies may be clowns, but their owners are also blessed with a good sense of humor.

Frenchies also like to ride and are pictured not only in cars but in wagons, carts, sleds, and baby carriages. And as often as not, they are pictured two together because Frenchies, being companions, like to do things together. Some Frenchies have also liked to pull carts as well as ride in them. It is obvious that the French Bulldogs and their owners like to entertain one another and anyone else within reach, and that they all like to have a good time.

The Frenchie may like a good time, but he can have his serious side, too. Frenchies, although not an easy breed to train, have made a very respectable showing in obedience. Dick Terrett was a strong believer in

Taking a picture is a group effort for these adorable Frenchies. The French Bulldog is a breed that enjoys the company of one another.

obedience titles and trained most of the dogs that lived with him. He put Companion Dog Obedience titles on numerous Terrett dogs, in addition to advanced degrees on three others. According to Terrett, most of the dogs were wonderful and willing to work, but a few were hard-headed and demanded a lot of patience.

Jack Vance put Utility degrees (UD) on two Frenchies, a difficult feat in any breed. In 1991, Andrea Morden-Moore's Frenchie became the fifth French Bulldog to earn a UD and since that date, Mike and Brenda Buckles have also placed a UD on a Frenchie. The Buckles have been very active in obedience work.

For obedience work, dog and handler need aptitude and determination. Having a dog that likes to please, like the Golden Retriever and the Labrador, is helpful. It has been said that training a dog in obedience teaches his master humility, in addition to teaching the dog to sit and stay. Once a degree is earned, there will be a tremendous feeling of accomplishment.

If you like to volunteer your time, taking your Frenchie to a nursing home once a week for several hours can be rewarding. The elder community loves to have a dog to visit with, and often your pet can bring a bit of companionship to someone who is either lonely or who may be feeling somewhat detached from the world. You will not only be bringing happiness to someone else, but researchers have discovered that volunteering helps to increase your longevity as well.

Although they are not the easiest breed to train, Frenchies have excelled in obedience. A well-behaved dog is a pleasure to have as a companion.

23

THE FRENCH BULLDOG STANDARD

Each breed approved by the American Kennel Club has a standard that gives the reader a mental picture of what the specific breed should look like. All reputable breeders strive to produce animals that will meet the requirements of this standard. In addition to having dogs that look like a proper French Bulldog, the standard ensures that the Frenchie will have the personality, disposition, and intelligence that is sought after in the breed.

As time progressed and breeders became more aware that certain attributes of the dog needed a better description or more definition, breeders would

According to the standard, the French Bulldog is an intelligent, muscular dog with an alert and interested expression.

meet and work to create a new standard. However, standards for any breed are never changed on a whim; serious study and exchange between breeders takes place before any revision is made.

THE OFFICIAL AKC STANDARD OF THE FRENCH BULLDOG

General Appearance—The French Bulldog has the appearance of an active, intelligent, muscular dog of heavy bone, smooth coat, compactly built, and of medium or small structure. Expression alert, curious, and interested. Any alteration other than removal of dewclaws is considered mutilation and is a *disqualification.*

Proportion and Symmetry—All points are well distributed and bear good relation one to the other; no feature being in such prominence from either excess or lack of quality that the animal appears poorly proportioned. ***Influence of Sex***—In comparing specimens of different sex, due allowance is to be made in favor of bitches, which do not bear the characteristics of the breed to the same marked degree as do the dogs.

Size, Proportion, Substance—***Weight*** not to exceed 28 pounds, over 28 pounds is a *disqualification.* ***Proportion***—Distance from withers to ground in good relation to distance from withers to onset of tail, so that animal appears compact, well balanced and in good proportion. ***Substance***-Muscular, heavy bone.

The French Bulldog's head is large and square with expressive eyes. Also prominent are the bat ears, which are broad at the base and elongated, set high on the head. Anything other than bat ears is a disqualification.

Head—*Head* large and square. **Eyes** dark in color wide apart, set low down in the skull, as far from the ears as possible, round in form, of moderate size, neither sunken nor bulging. In lighter colored dogs, lighter colored eyes are acceptable. No haw and no white of the eye showing when looking forward. **Ears**—Known as the bat ear, broad at the base, elongated, with round top, set high on the head but not too close together, and carried erect with the orifice to the front. The leather of the ear fine and soft. Other than bat ears is a *disqualification.*

The top of the **skull** flat between the ears, the forehead is not flat but slightly rounded. The **muzzle** broad, deep and well laid back; the muscles of the cheeks well developed. The *stop* well defined, causing a hollow groove between the eyes with heavy wrinkles forming; a soft roll over the extremely short nose; nostrils broad with a well defined line between them. **Nose** black. Nose other than black is a *disqualification,* except in the case of the lighter colored dogs, where a lighter colored nose is acceptable but not desirable. *Flews* black, thick and broad, hanging over the lower jaw at the sides, meeting the underlip in front and covering the teeth, which are not seen when the mouth is closed. The *underjaw* is deep, square, broad, undershot and well turned up.

Neck, Topline, Body—The **neck** is thick and well arched with loose skin at the throat. The **back** is a roach back with a slight fall close behind the shoul-

This French Bulldog demonstrates the proper proportions for the breed. His body is short and muscular with a broad, deep chest.

ders; strong and short, broad at the shoulder and narrowing at the loins. The **body** is short and well rounded. The *chest* is broad, deep, and full; well ribbed with the belly tucked up. The **tail** is either straight or screwed (but not curly), short, hung low, thick root and fine tip; carried low in repose.

Forequarters—*Forelegs* are short, stout, straight, muscular and set wide apart. Dewclaws may be removed. *Feet* are moderate in size, compact and firmly set. Toes compact, well split up, with high knuckles and short stubby nails.

Hindquarters—*Hind legs* are strong and muscular, longer than the forelegs, so as to elevate the loins above the shoulders. Hocks well let down. *Feet* are moderate in size, compact and firmly set. Toes compact, well split up, with high knuckles and short stubby nails; hind feet slightly longer than forefeet.

Coat—Coat is moderately fine, brilliant, short and smooth. Skin is soft and loose, especially at the head and shoulder, forming wrinkles.

Something must be interesting in there. As this Frenchie shows, strong, muscular hindlegs are a common characteristic of the unique breed.

Color—Acceptable colors—All brindle, fawn, white, brindle and white, and any color except those which constitute disqualification. All colors are acceptable with the exception of solid black, mouse, liver, black and tan, black and white, and white with black, which are *disqualifications.* Black means black without a trace of brindle.

Gait—Correct gait is double tracking with reach and drive; the action is unrestrained, free and vigorous.

Temperament—Well behaved, adaptable, and comfortable companions with an affectionate nature and even disposition, generally active, alert, and playful, but not unduly boisterous.

Part of a Frenchie's appeal is his smooth coat, which ranges in colors from brindle to white.

DISQUALIFICATIONS

Any alteration other than removal of dewclaws.
Over 28 pounds in weight.
Other than bat ears.
Nose other than black, except in the case of lighter colored dogs, where a lighter colored nose is acceptable. Solid black, mouse, liver, black and tan, black and white, and white with black. Black means black without a trace of brindle.
Approved June 10, 1991
Effective July 31, 1991

BRINGING YOUR FRENCHIE HOME

The French Bulldog is not an easily attainable breed, so you may have to wait up to six months for a puppy.

You have done your research on the French Bulldog and have decided that this is the breed that will fit into your household. You may have attended one or two dog shows in your area, not only to get a better look at the breed but to meet some of the breeders. You have also stopped at your local library to look through the canine reference books to see what they have to say about the breed. You are aware of the health problems in the breed, you have decided if you want a male or a female, and you have contacted some reputable breeders in regard to purchasing your puppy. The French Bulldog is not a popular breed, like the Poodle or the Golden Retriever, so you may have to wait up to six months or more for a puppy to become available. Be patient. This is a major

purchase, not only in terms of money but also in energy and time. This is like bringing a child into your household, except that this addition will always remain a child!

You have finally found a breeder that will be producing a litter and you have made your deposit on a puppy. He will probably be coming home with you when he is about 12 weeks old.

The breeder will talk to you before you pick up your puppy, and she will tell you what kind of dog food to buy. This will be a food that she has been feeding the puppies and it will probably be a combination of moist and dry puppy chow. It is best to keep your dog on the same food that he has been eating, as this will minimize stomach problems when he arrives in his new home. You will also want to buy a leash and collar. Your breeder can tell you what kind and size will be best for the Frenchie. Buy two pans, one for water and one for food. You should also purchase a crate. Some people think that dog crates are "cruel" but on the contrary, they become a safe haven for your dog—his home. And without a doubt, a crate will save much wear and tear on your house. Your local pet mart can tell you what size crate you should have for a 20- to 28-pound dog.

Nutrition plays a very important role in a dog's growth process. Keeping your Frenchie puppy on his original diet will help minimize stomach problems when he arrives in his new home.

A dog crate is very useful when traveling with your new puppy. Be sure to line the crate with some towels or a blanket and bring a few toys to keep your curious puppy occupied.

Do not let your Frenchie run lose at any time. If you do not have a fenced back yard, you must walk your dog on a leash or keep him in an exercise pen when he is outside. Frenchies are really house dogs—they have little desire to spend hours outdoors, although they do like to sleep in a sunbeam in nice weather.

The big day finally arrives, and you are ready to bring your new family member home. Talk to your breeder and see when it would be convenient for you to pick up the newcomer. Usually a Saturday or Sunday morning is the best time, because you will have a full day or two to get your pup acclimatized to his surroundings and family members.

If the trip is several hours from your home, you may want to take the dog crate with you. Use a few towels or a blanket for bedding and be sure to bring a pan so that your puppy can have a drink of water if he gets warm. If it is a short trip, you can count on someone holding the new baby. You may also have to exercise your pup if the trip takes more than two hours, so be sure to bring the leash along. Remember, under no circumstances can you let your dog run loose! You should also carry several plastic bags so that you can pick up any feces and discard them in a trash container. It is important that all dog owners show responsibility while exercising their dogs, regardless of where they are.

When you arrive home, put your dog in the yard first so that he can relieve himself and be sure to praise him. It is highly unlikely that he will arrive housebroken—wishful thinking!

Let him explore his new surroundings and give him a light meal and a pan of water. When your puppy appears tired, place him in his crate, close the door, and let him sleep either for a couple of hours if it is daytime or for the night if it is bedtime.

Try to keep the first 48 hours fairly quiet for the puppy. Let him get used to his new home and family before bringing friends and relatives in to meet him. Everything is new to him at this point, and there is no reason to overwhelm him with additional distractions. Be sure to take him outside as soon as you take him out of his crate. This will make your housebreaking job much easier.

DOG PROOFING YOUR HOME

You should be aware of some of the dangers facing a puppy in the home and yard. Think of it in terms of a toddler poking his head and fingers into all kinds of spots and openings that could be hazardous.

It's important that children are taught how to hold a fragile puppy the proper way. They must understand that a puppy is not a toy and has to be handled carefully. Here, Mark and "Trouble" demonstrate the correct way to handle a small pup.

The French Bulldog has an easygoing and lovable personality, which makes living in a multi-dog household comfortable and peaceful.

A swimming pool or pond can be very dangerous for a dog, whether puppy or adult. In particular, dogs that have fairly short legs and are heavy bodied, such as the French Bulldog, can easily drown in a pool. Be certain that your dog cannot get into the pool or fall into it and drown. Not all dogs can swim and worse yet, many dogs cannot get out of a pool without assistance.

Puppies love to chew on wires, so be sure electrical cords are off the floor and hidden from view. Check to see that your pup can't fall through the railings on your deck or balcony. Use your common sense and be aware where dangers may lie. Even if you feel you have everything out of the way, you may be surprised at what they can find to get into. If this is the first dog in your home, small children must also be taught how to care for the new puppy. They must be taught how to pick the dog up and how to carry him properly. They must also be taught that they cannot ride on the dog, pull his ears, drag him around the house, or drop him. They must also understand that the puppy cannot be dropped. If young children can be taught all of this at an early age, they will become lifelong, compassionate animal owners and animal lovers. Do not leave your children alone with the puppy until you are sure that they will treat him well.

Your new puppy must be introduced to the other pets in your home. If you have a cat that has never seen a dog before, your cat will also need some special attention and probably some coaxing for a few days to get him to come out from behind the furnace. If your cat still has his claws, you must be very careful that he does not scratch the Frenchie's eyes. If you have an elderly dog, make sure that the puppy doesn't unduly pester him.

SPECIAL CONCERNS

French Bulldogs are very susceptible to heat and cold due to their short noses, large soft palates, and heavily muscled throats that create respiratory difficulties under the best of conditions. If it is a hot day, keep your dog where air is circulating, give him plenty of water, and be sure to avoid exercise (such as walks) and excitement. An air-conditioned, draft-free room is best, but if you don't have air conditioning, an oscillating fan will work very well. Never leave your dog in a car in the sun. Do not leave your dog outside without ample shade and a water dish.

If your dog begins to vomit or breathe rapidly and heavily and cannot stand, suspect heat prostration. Place your dog in the bathtub or spray him down with a hose immediately. You want to wet down the stomach and legs first as this is where the large veins are located. Keep him in the water until he appears to no longer be distressed. If you are still concerned about him, call your veterinarian.

You must also guard your dog against extreme cold. The Frenchie is a short-coated breed that doesn't have much covering against the elements. If you are taking your Frenchie for a walk on a cold day, you may want to put a jacket on him. He will look very smart and be warm, too. Again, do not leave your dog outside for

The first few weeks in a strange home may be difficult for a small puppy. Providing your Frenchie with a warm bed and some cuddly toys can help him feel safe and secure.

Make sure that you take your dog outside after every meal to relieve himself. Praise and positive reinforcement are a very big part of the housebreaking process.

more than a few minutes when the temperature is very cold.

THE FIRST NIGHT

The first night or two in his new home may be difficult for both the family and the puppy. He is used to being with his many siblings, used to his mother, and used to his breeder. Now, he finds himself all alone with people that he does not know. A teddy bear or a fuzzy sweater can be of comfort to a puppy in new surroundings. A ticking clock near the crate also helps and sometimes a small nightlight will comfort him. You can also try leaving a radio on playing quiet music in the room.

Give your puppy some extra attention on his first night, and if he should cry or whimper, let him be and he will soon settle down. Do not take your puppy to bed with you—leave him in his crate. The second night should be easier for all of you, and by the third night he should settle right in at bedtime.

HOUSEBREAKING

Housetraining is very important and you must begin to train your dog as soon as you bring him home. Every time the puppy wakes up he must be quickly taken outside. Watch him and as soon as he urinates or defecates, praise him, "Good dog, good boy," and give him a pat on the head. He undoubtedly will have a few accidents at first, but he should learn fairly quickly what is expected of him. You must use diligence. A big part of housebreaking is training yourself to know the dog's habits. In addition to putting him outside when he wakes up, he must go out as soon as he has eaten and after he has played for a while. You can often catch your puppy circling around, which is a clue that he needs to go outdoors. A crate is a major help in housebreaking because puppies will usually not soil the area that they sleep in. In addition, it is easy to run the pup outside as soon as you take him out of his crate. Frenchies are quite smart and fairly easy to train, so within a short period of time your dog will be housetrained. Remember, though, that accidents will periodically happen and the pup should be forgiven.

IDENTIFICATION

It would be a very good idea for your dog to have permanent identification in the form of a microchip. The chip is the size of a grain of rice and is injected between the dog's shoulder blades. The dog feels no discomfort and it only takes a few seconds for a veterinarian to insert it. The number on the chip is then registered with a national organization, such as the American Kennel Club. Nearly all humane societies and veterinarians have a scanner whereby they can scan the chip, get the number, and locate the owner of the dog. This will be money well spent. You may also have your dog tattooed on the inner rear leg or the ear with your social security number. I have an eight-year-old French Bulldog with a tattoo, but at his age it is barely legible. My younger Frenchie has a microchip, and I feel that this is a much better form of permanent identification.

All dogs should have some sort of identification on them in case of an emergency.

FEEDING YOUR FRENCH BULLDOG

Dog owners today are fortunate that they live in an age when considerable money has been invested in the study of canine nutritional requirements. Major dog food manufacturers are concerned about ensuring that their foods are of the best quality and of the best nutritional value. Many dog food manufacturers have representatives at local dog shows and they are always available to answer any questions that you may have about their product.

Once your puppy is off of his puppy chow, usually around six or eight months of age, you may want to advance to the adult food of the brand that you have been using, or you may want to change to another brand. At this time, you should probably either consult

Fortunately, a lot of research has been conducted on dog food and proper nutrition. If you are not sure what kind of food or how much to feed your Frenchie, consult the breeder or your veterinarian.

the breeder of your puppy or your veterinarian for suggestions as to what brand will be best for your dog. This is also a good time to start reading the labels on dog food bags to see the nutritional value, caloric value, protein, and fat contents of the brand. A good compromise on your dog's diet is to feed him moistened, dried chow mixed with a small amount of canned food. If your dog is very active, you will have to feed him more than if he is fairly sedentary. Be sure to always have fresh water available for your dog.

When your Frenchie was a puppy, you were probably feeding him three or four times a day. As he grows into adulthood you will start feeding him twice a day, once in the morning and once in the evening. You will be surprised that as your dog reaches adulthood, he will be eating less in a day than he did when he was a young puppy and his bones and body were growing at a rapid rate.

French Bulldogs should not exceed 28 pounds in weight if they are to be shown. Any dog over this weight will be disqualified. Some Frenchies mature at around 26 pounds, and it can be very easy to add another 2 or 3 pounds onto his frame if you are not strict about diet. In addition to not wanting an overweight dog for the show ring, it is important to keep a Frenchie's weight in check for health reasons. An overweight dog, just like an overweight person, will

Monitor your dog's weight closely, because you do not want it to exceed the normal limit. An overweight dog can develop health problems.

later develop back problems, heart problems, and just plain difficulty in moving around. Do not burden your Frenchie with any extra poundage.

A word of warning—Frenchies love to eat. The breeder of my dogs, a French woman, once said to me, "Mais oui! Le Bouledogue Francais has a *sophisticated* palate!—and indeed he has!" Steve Eltinge, in his beautiful and informative book, *The French Bulldog*, wrote "If your French Bulldog was capable of expressing its fondest culinary desires you would be enlisted to have on hand, at all times, a menu consisting of fromage, filet mignon, poulet a l'ail, la pasta et la beurre, patisserie, gateaux et creme. Of course, only one meal per day would be an insult and two barely sufficient....They do love their stomachs."

When planning your dog's diet, feed a reputable brand of dog food, keep the table scraps and treats to a minimum as poundage increases rapidly with a tidbit every few hours, keep fresh water available at all times, and use your common sense.

FACTORS AFFECTING NUTRITIONAL NEEDS

Activity Level. A dog that lives in a country environment and is able to exercise for long periods of the day will need more food than the same breed of dog living in an apartment and given little exercise.

Quality of the Food. Obviously the quality of food will affect the quantity required by a puppy. If the nutritional content of a food is low then the puppy will need more of it than if a better quality food was fed.

Balance of Nutrients and Vitamins. Feeding a puppy the correct balance of nutrients is not easy because the average person is not able to measure

The amount of exercise your Frenchie receives affects his food intake. A dog that has a lot of space to play in will need more to eat than a dog that lives in a more confined space, such as in an apartment.

out ratios of one to another, so it is a case of trying to see that nothing is in excess. However, only tests, or your veterinarian, can be the source of reliable advice.

Genetic and Biological Variation. Apart from all of the other considerations, it should be remembered that each puppy is an individual. His genetic make-up will influence not only his physical characteristics but also his metabolic efficiency. This being so, two pups from the same litter can vary quite a bit in the amount of food they need to perform the same function under the same conditions. If you consider the potential combinations of all of these factors then you will see that pups of a given breed could vary quite a bit in the amount of food they will need. Before discussing feeding quantities it is valuable to know at least a little about the composition of food and its role in the body.

COMPOSITION AND ROLE OF FOOD

The main ingredients of food are protein, fats, and carbohydrates, each of which is needed in relatively

The amount of food your French Bulldog requires will depend on his age and level of activity. This Frenchie will need less food than a more active dog.

large quantities when compared to the other needs of vitamins and minerals. The other vital ingredient of food is, of course, water. Although all foods obviously contain some of the basic ingredients needed for an animal to survive, they do not all contain the ingredients in the needed ratios or type. For example, there are many forms of protein, just as there are many types of carbohydrates. Both of these compounds are found in meat and in vegetable matter—but not all of those that are needed will be in one particular meat or vegetable. Plants, especially, do not contain certain amino acids that are required for the synthesis of certain proteins needed by dogs.

Likewise, vitamins are found in meats and vegetable matter, but vegetables are a richer source of most. Meat contains very little carbohydrates. Some vitamins can be synthesized by the dog, so do not need to be supplied via the food. Dogs are carnivores and this means their digestive tract has evolved to need a high quantity of meat as compared to humans. The digestive system of carnivores is unable to break down the tough cellulose walls of plant matter, but it is easily able to assimilate proteins from meat.

In order to gain its needed vegetable matter in a form that it can cope with, the carnivore eats all of its prey. This includes the partly digested food within the stomach. In commercially prepared foods, the cellulose is broken down by cooking. During this process the vitamin content is either greatly reduced or lost altogether. The manufacturer therefore adds vitamins once the heat process has been completed. This is why commercial foods are so useful as part of a feeding regimen, providing they are of good quality and from a company that has prepared the foods very carefully.

Proteins

These are made from amino acids, of which at least ten are essential if a puppy is to maintain healthy growth. Proteins provide the building blocks for the puppy's body. The richest sources are meat, fish and poultry, together with their by-products. The latter will include milk, cheese, yogurt, fishmeal, and eggs. Vegetable matter that has a high protein content includes soy beans, together with numerous corn and other plant extracts that have been dehydrated. The actual protein content needed in the diet

Meats, fish, and poultry are good sources of protein, which provide the building blocks for your puppy's body.

will be determined both by the activity level of the dog and his age. The total protein need will also be influenced by the digestibility factor of the food given.

Fats

These serve numerous roles in the puppy's body. They provide insulation against the cold, and help buffer the organs from knocks and general activity shocks. They provide the richest source of energy, and reserves of this, and they are vital in the transport of vitamins and other nutrients, via the blood, to all other organs. Finally, it is the fat content within a diet that gives it palatability. It is important that the fat content of a diet should not be excessive. This is because the high energy content of fats (more than twice that of protein or carbohydrate) will increase the overall energy content of the diet. The puppy will adjust its food intake to that of its energy needs, which are obviously more easily met in a high-energy diet. This will mean that while the fats are providing the energy needs of the puppy, the over-all diet may not be providing its protein, vitamin, and mineral needs, so signs of protein deficiency will become apparent. Rich sources of fats are meat, their byproducts (butter, milk), and vegetable oils, such as safflower, olive, corn or soy bean.

Carbohydrates

These are the principal energy compounds given to puppies and adult dogs. Their inclusion within most commercial brand dog foods is for cost, rather than dietary needs. These compounds are more commonly known as sugars, and they are seen in simple or complex compounds of carbon, hydrogen, and oxygen. One of the simple sugars is called glucose, and it is vital to many metabolic processes. When large chains of glucose are created, they form compound sugars. One of these is called glycogen, and it is found in the cells of animals. Another, called starch, is the material that is found in the cells of plants.

Vitamins

These are not foods as such but chemical compounds that assist in all aspects of an animal's life. They help in so many ways that to attempt to describe these effectively would require a chapter in itself. Fruits are a rich source of vitamins, as is the liver of most animals. Many vitamins are unstable and easily destroyed by light, heat, moisture, or rancidity. An excess of vitamins, especially A and D, has been proven to be very harmful. Provided a puppy is receiving a balanced diet, it is most unlikely there will be a deficiency, whereas hypervitaminosis (an excess of vitamins) has become quite common due to owners and breeders feeding unneeded supplements. The only time you should feed extra vitamins to your puppy is if your veterinarian advises you to.

Your puppy will depend on you to meet his nutritional needs once he arrives in your home.

Minerals

These provide strength to bone and cell tissue, as well as assist in many metabolic processes. Examples are calcium, phosphorous, copper, iron, magnesium, selenium, potassium, zinc, and sodium. The recommended amounts of all minerals in the diet has not been fully established. Calcium and phosphorous are known to be important, especially to puppies. They help in forming strong bone. As with vitamins, a mineral deficiency is most unlikely in pups given a good and varied diet. Again, an excess can create problems—this applying equally to calcium.

Water

This is the most important of all nutrients, as is easily shown by the fact that the adult dog is made up of about 60 percent water, the puppy containing an even higher percentage. Dogs must retain a water balance, which means that the total intake should be balanced by the total output. The intake comes either by direct input (the tap or its equivalent), plus water released when food is oxidized, known as metabolic water (remember that all foods contain the elements hydrogen and oxygen that recombine in the body to create water). A dog without adequate water will lose condition more rapidly than one depleted of food, a fact common to most animal species.

AMOUNT TO FEED

The best way to determine dietary requirements is by observing the puppy's general health and physical appearance. If he is well covered with flesh, shows good bone development and muscle, and is an active alert puppy, then his diet is fine. A puppy will consume about twice as much as an adult (of the same breed). You should ask the breeder of your puppy to show you the amounts fed to their pups and this will be a good starting point.

The puppy should eat his meal in about five to seven minutes. Any leftover food can be discarded or placed into the refrigerator until the next meal (but be sure it is thawed fully if your fridge is very cold).

If the puppy quickly devours his meal and is clearly still hungry, then you are not giving him enough food. If he eats readily but then begins to pick at it, or walks away leaving a quantity, then you are probably giving him too much food. Adjust this at the next meal and you will quickly begin to appreciate what the correct amount is. If, over a number of weeks, the pup starts to look fat, then he is obviously overeating; the reverse is true if he starts to look thin compared with others of the same breed.

WHEN TO FEED

It really does not matter what times of the day the puppy is fed, as long as he receives the needed quantity of food. Puppies from 8 weeks to 12 or 16 weeks need 3 or 4 meals a day. Older puppies and adult dogs should be fed twice a day. What is most important is that the feeding times are reasonably regular. They can be tailored to fit in with your own timetable—for example, 7 a.m. and 6 p.m. The dog will then expect his meals at these times each day. Keeping regular feeding times and feeding set amounts will help you monitor your puppy's or dog's health. If a dog that's normally enthusiastic about mealtimes and eats readily suddenly shows a lack of interest in food, you'll know something's not right.

A healthy puppy is a happy puppy. Establishing a feeding schedule with set amounts of food will help you monitor your Frenchie's health.

GROOMING YOUR FRENCH BULLDOG

Understand that when you purchase a dog, you have the responsibility of maintaining your pet. Think of it in terms of having a child—you bathe your youngster, comb his hair, and put a clean set of clothes on him. The end result is that you have a child that smells good, looks nice, and that you enjoy having in your company. It is the same with your dog—keep the dog brushed and clean and you will find it a pleasure to be in his company. Fortunately, owners of a French Bulldog have a minimum of grooming compared to owners of heavily groomed terriers like the Scottish Terrier.

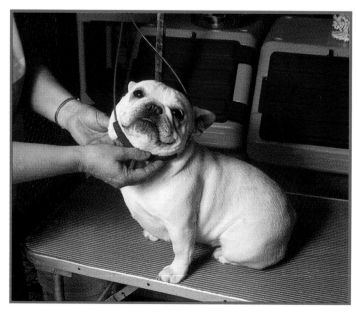

There are certain tools that you should have in order to make grooming time easier and more comfortable for your dog, such as a grooming table with a "hangar."

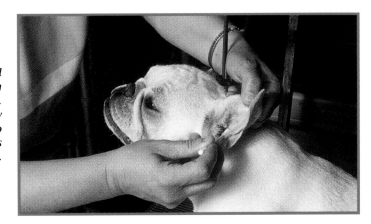

Cotton swabs are a good tool to use for cleaning your Frenchie's ears. Remember to be very gentle so as not to puncture or harm his eardrum.

Grooming will primarily consist of a weekly "go-over."

Here are the tools that you will need for grooming:

1. A grooming table, something sturdy with a rubber mat covering the top. You will need a grooming arm or a "hangar." (You can use a table in your laundry room with an eye hook in the ceiling to hold the leash.) Your dog will be comfortable even if confined, and you will be able to work on the dog. Grooming (especially when trimming toenails) can be a frustrating job if you try to groom without a table and a grooming arm.

2. A rubber brush or a grooming glove and a toenail trimmer.

3. Cotton balls, swabs, and old washcloths.

To start: Set your dog on the table and put a leash around his neck. Have the leash up behind the ears and make the leash taut when you fasten it to your eye hook or to the hangar. Do not walk away and leave your dog unattended, because he could jump off of the table and be left dangling from the leash with his feet scrambling around in the air.

Brush him out and wipe him down with a damp washcloth. Check his eyes and clean them with a damp cotton ball. Check the ears and use a swab dipped in alcohol to gently clean them. Always check for any unusual lumps or bumps when grooming your dog.

If your dog needs a bath, put him in the laundry tub and give him a good scrub and rinsing. After toweling him down, return him to the grooming table. This is a good time to trim toenails, because they will be soft and easier to cut after the dog is bathed. You will also find that a bath will loosen any dead coat, so after bathing be sure to brush him out thoroughly to clean out any dead undercoat. You can dry your dog with a hair dryer and brush him again, or you can let him dry naturally and then brush him out.

You may want to trim the whiskers to the skin as this will give your dog a neat, clean-cut look. Wipe him dry with a towel or use a hair dryer. If it is a nice, sunny day, you many want to put him on the deck to dry.

If you are showing your French Bulldog, you can rub him down with a pomade to give his coat a high gloss. In addition, a twice weekly brushing (along with a healthy diet) will keep the coat shiny. Trimming for show will be very minimal, the purpose being to give a neat appearance. Pluck any of the few out-of-place hairs with your fingers. If showing, be sure to trim the face whiskers.

Voila! You are finished! Smooth-coated dogs are low maintenance and those of us who own one appreciate it.

Of course, if you want to take the easy way out, you can eliminate all of the grooming for yourself and take your dog to the groomer every couple of months to have him bathed, dried, and his toenails trimmed. However, when you have a breed that is as easy to groom as the French Bulldog, it seems a shame to leave the job up to someone else.

To wrap it up, your pet should be brushed weekly and bathed as needed. The toenails should be trimmed every month or so. Follow this easy plan and your dog will be clean, he will smell good, and it will be a pleasure to be in his company.

To maintain an overall neat appearance, you should trim your Frenchie's toenails about every month or so. Beginning grooming at an early age will help your dog to feel more comfortable.

TRAINING YOUR FRENCH BULLDOG

Every French Bulldog expects to be able to lie around the house, have a good meal, receive love and attention, and be taken for a walk or a romp every day. However, some owners like the challenge of working with their dog and of training him to follow commands. And, believe it or not, some French Bulldogs are ready to move away from their sunbeam and do a little work!

Frenchies are not an easy breed to work with in obedience, but many have earned their Companion Degrees so it is not an impossible task. However, it is worthwhile for every dog owner to train his dog in the very basic commands. If your dog ever gets off leash and makes a dash for the street, the come command will be a lifesaver. Basic obedience, will at least give your dog enough manners to be a gentleman or a lady when company is in the house.

Obedience classes are offered throughout the country and unless you live in a very remote area, your town or city should offer you a selection of training clubs. There are different methods of instruction and you may find it helpful to visit various classes to see which method of training you prefer.

You will usually start training your pup at about six months of age. Classes will meet once or twice a week for six to ten weeks. Having successfully completed one of these classes (and success means passing the examination at the end of the class), you should have a dog that will sit on command, come when called, and walk decently on a lead. This is all that many dog owners require. They want a pet that

Basic training can begin at six months of age. To help the process along, you can enroll your Frenchie in a puppy kindergarten class, which usually lasts from six to ten weeks.

behaves like a gentleman or a lady. If you have never owned a dog before or never owned a dog with good manners, obedience class work may be just what you want and need.

At their national specialties, The French Bulldog Club of America offers classes in obedience, and entries are usually between 15 and 20. All classes will usually have entries in Novice, Open, and Utility. Angel and Richard Terrette have by far been the most active breeders with dogs in obedience work, putting a Companion Dog degree on seven Frenchies, Companion Dog Excellent on three dogs, and Utility Dog on Ch. Terrette's Tigre le Chasseur. At the present time, there are several other individuals who are very active in obedience work.

COLLAR AND LEASH TRAINING

Training a puppy to his collar and leash is very easy. Place a collar on the puppy and, although he will initially try to bite at it, he will soon forget it, the more so if you play with him. You can leave the collar on for a few hours. Some people leave their dogs' collars on all of the time, others only when they are taking the dog out. If it is to be left on, purchase a narrow or round one so it does not mark the fur.

Once the puppy ignores his collar, then you can attach the leash to it and let the puppy pull this along behind it for a few minutes. However, if the pup starts to chew at the leash, simply hold the leash but keep it slack and let the pup go where he wants. The idea is to let him get the feel of the leash, but not get in the habit of chewing it. Repeat this a couple of times a day for two days and the pup will get used to the leash without thinking that it will restrain him—which you will not have attempted to do yet.

Next, you can let the pup understand that the leash will restrict his movements. The first time he realizes this, he will pull and buck or just sit down. Immediately call the pup to you and give him lots of fuss. Never tug on the leash so the puppy is dragged along the floor, as this simply implants a negative thought in his mind.

THE COME COMMAND

Come is the most vital of all commands and especially so for the independently minded dog. To teach the puppy to come, let him reach the end of a long lead, then give the command and his name, gently pulling him toward you at the same time. As soon as he associates the word come with the action of moving toward you, pull only when he does not respond immediately. As he starts to come, move

At first, your puppy may be annoyed with a leash and collar and try to bite it. Eventually, he will learn to ignore it.

back to make him learn that he must come from a distance as well as when he is close to you. Soon you may be able to practice without a leash, but if he is slow to come or notably disobedient, go to him and pull him toward you, repeating the command. Never scold a dog during this exercise—or any other exercise. Remember the trick is that the puppy must want to come to you. For the very independent dog, hand signals may work better than verbal commands.

THE SIT COMMAND

As with most basic commands, your puppy will learn this one in just a few lessons. You can give the puppy two lessons a day on the sit command but he will make just as much progress with one 15-minute lesson each day. Some trainers will advise you that you should not proceed to other commands until the previous one has been learned really well. However, a bright young pup is quite capable of handling more than one command per lesson, and certainly per day. Indeed, as time progresses, you will be going through each command as a matter of routine before a new one is attempted. This is so the puppy always starts, as well as ends, a lesson on a high note, having successfully completed something.

Call the puppy to you and fuss over him. Place one hand on his hindquarters and the other under his upper chest. Say "Sit" in a pleasant (never harsh) voice. At the same time, push down his rear end and push up under his chest. Now lavish praise on the puppy. Repeat this a few times and your pet will get the idea. Once the puppy is in the sit position you will release your hands. At first he will tend to get up, so immediately repeat the exercise. The lesson will end when the pup is in the sit position. When the puppy understands the command, and does it right away, you can slowly move backwards so that you are a few feet away from him. If he attempts to come to you, simply place him back in the original position and start again. Do not attempt to keep the pup in the sit position for too long. At this age, even a few seconds is a long while and you do not want him to get bored with lessons before he has even begun them.

THE HEEL COMMAND

All dogs should be able to walk nicely on a leash without their owners being involved in a tug-of-war.

The sit command is the foundation for all other commands. It teaches your dog self-control and he learns that good things, such as treats and praise, come to dogs that can sit nicely.

The heel command will follow leash training. Heel training is best done where you have a wall to one side of you. This will restrict the puppy's lateral movements, so you only have to contend with forward and backward situations. A fence is an alternative, or you can do the lesson in the garage. Again, it is better to do the lesson in private, not on a public sidewalk where there will be many distractions.

With a puppy, there will be no need to use a choke collar as you can be just as effective with a regular one. The leash should be of good length, certainly not too short. You can adjust the space between you, the puppy, and the wall so your pet has only a small amount of room to move sideways. This being so, he will either hang back or pull ahead—the latter is the more desirable state as it indicates a bold pup who is not frightened of you.

Hold the leash in your right hand and pass it through your left. As the puppy moves ahead and strains on the leash, give the leash a quick jerk backwards with your left hand, at the same time saying "Heel." The position you want the pup to be in is such that his chest is level with, or just behind, an imaginary line from your knee. When the puppy is in this position, praise him and begin walking again, and the whole exercise will be repeated. Once the puppy begins to get the message, you can use your left hand to pat the side of your knee so the pup is encouraged to keep close to your side.

It is useful to suddenly do an about-turn when the pup understands the basics. The puppy will now be behind you, so you can pat your knee and say "Heel." As soon as the pup is in the correct position, give him lots of praise. The puppy will now be beginning to associate certain words with certain actions. Whenever he is not in the heel position he will experience displeasure as you jerk the leash, but when he comes alongside you he will receive praise. Given these two options, he will always prefer the latter—assuming he has no other reason to fear you, which would then create a dilemma in his mind.

Once the lesson has been well learned, then you can adjust your pace from a slow walk to a quick one and the puppy will come to adjust. The slow walk is always the more difficult for most puppies, as they are usually anxious to be on the move.

If you have no wall to walk against then things will be a little more difficult because the pup will tend to wander to his left. This means you need to give lateral jerks as well as bring the pup to your side. End the lesson when the pup is walking nicely beside you. Begin the lesson with a few sit commands (which he understands by now), so you're starting with success and praise. If your puppy is nervous on the leash, you should never drag him to your side as you may see so many other people do (who obviously didn't invest in a good book like you did!). If the pup sits down, call him to your side and give lots of praise. The pup must always come to you because he wants to. If he is dragged to your side he will see you doing the dragging—a big negative. When he races ahead he does not see you jerk the leash, so all he knows is that something restricted his movement and, once he was in a given position, you gave him lots of praise. This is using canine psychology to your advantage.

Always try to remember that if a dog must be disciplined, then try not to let him associate the discipline with you. This is not possible in all matters but, where it is, this is definitely to be preferred.

Opposite: Training your Frenchie will require time and patience. Don't proceed to the next lesson until he has successfully completed the previous exercise.

THE STAY COMMAND

This command follows from the sit. Face the puppy and say "Sit." Now step backwards, and as you do, say "Stay." Let the pup remain in the position for only a few seconds before calling him to you and giving lots of praise. Repeat this, but step further back. You do not need to shout at the puppy. Your pet is not deaf;

in fact, his hearing is far better than yours. Speak just loudly enough for the pup to hear, yet use a firm voice. You can stretch the word to form a "sta-a-a-y." If the pup gets up and comes to you simply lift him up, place him back in the original position, and start again. As the pup comes to understand the command, you can move further and further back.

The next test is to walk away after placing the pup. This will mean your back is to him, which will tempt him to follow you. Keep an eye over your shoulder, and the minute the pup starts to move, spin around and, using a sterner voice, say either "Sit" or "Stay." If the pup has gotten quite close to you, then, again, return him to the original position.

As the weeks go by you can increase the length of time the pup is left in the stay position—but two to three minutes is quite long enough for a puppy. If your puppy drops into a lying position and is clearly more comfortable, there is nothing wrong with this. Likewise, your pup will want to face the direction in which you walked off. Some trainers will insist that the dog faces the direction he was placed in, regardless of whether you move off on his blind side. I have never believed in this sort of obedience because it has no practical benefit.

Once your Frenchie can sit properly, teach him how to stay in position until you release him.

THE DOWN COMMAND

From the puppy's viewpoint, the down command can be one of the more difficult ones to accept. This is because the position is one taken up by a submissive dog in a wild pack situation. A timid dog will roll over—a natural gesture of submission. A bolder pup will want to get up, and might back off, not feeling he should have to submit to this command. He will feel that he is under attack from you and about to be punished—which is what would be the position in his natural environment. Once he comes to understand this is not the case, he will accept this unnatural position without any problem.

Because dogs do not like to be in a submissive position, the down command may be difficult for him to master. Lefox Cherie Clair de Lune looks pretty comfortable lying down on her master's lap.

You may notice that some dogs will sit very quickly, but will respond to the down command more slowly—it is their way of saying that they will obey the command, but under protest!

There two ways to teach this command. One is, in my mind, more intimidating than the other, but it is up to you to decide which one works best for you. The first method is to stand in front of your puppy and bring

him to the sit position, with his collar and leash on. Pass the leash under your left foot so that when you pull on it, the result is that the pup's neck is forced downwards. With your free left hand, push the pup's shoulders down while at the same time saying "Down." This is when a bold pup will instantly try to back off and wriggle in full protest. Hold the pup firmly by the shoulders so he stays in the position for a second or two, then tell him what a good dog he is and give him lots of praise. Repeat this only a few times in a lesson because otherwise the puppy will get bored and upset over this command. End with an easy command that brings back the pup's confidence.

The second method, and the one I prefer, is done as follows: Stand in front of the pup and then tell him to sit. Now kneel down, which is immediately far less intimidating to the puppy than to have you towering above him. Take each of his front legs and pull them forward, at the same time saying "Down." Release the legs and quickly apply light pressure on the shoulders with your left hand. Then, as quickly, say "Good boy" and give lots of fuss. Repeat two or three times only. The pup will learn over a few lessons. Remember, this is a very submissive act on the pup's behalf, so there is no need to rush matters.

RECALL TO HEEL COMMAND

When your puppy is coming to the heel position from an off-leash situation—such as if he has been running free—he should do this in the correct manner. He should pass behind you and take up his position and then sit. To teach this command, have the pup in front of you in the sit position with his collar and leash on. Hold the leash in your right hand. Give him the command to heel, and pat your left knee. As the pup starts to move forward, use your right hand to guide him behind you. If need be you can hold his collar and walk the dog around the back of you to the desired position. You will need to repeat this a few times until the dog understands what is wanted.

When he has done this a number of times, you can try it without the collar and leash. If the pup comes up toward your left side, then bring him to the sit position in front of you, hold his collar and walk him around the back of you. He will eventually understand and automatically pass around your back each time. If the dog is already behind you when you recall him, then he should automatically come to your left side, which you will be patting with your hand.

THE NO COMMAND

This is a command that must be obeyed every time without fail. There are no halfway stages, he must be 100-percent reliable. Most delinquent dogs have never been taught this command; included in these are the jumpers, the barkers, and the biters. Were your puppy to approach a poisonous snake or any other potential danger, the no command, coupled with the recall, could save his life. You do not need to give a specific lesson for this command because it will crop up time and again in day-to-day life.

If the puppy is chewing a slipper, you should approach the pup, take hold of the slipper, and say "No" in a stern voice. If he jumps onto the furniture, lift him off and say "No" and place him gently on the floor. You must be consistent in the use of the command and apply it every time he is doing something you do not want him to do.

Be firm and consistent when teaching your Frenchie the no command. It could help save his life one day.

SHOWING YOUR FRENCH BULLDOG

Dog shows have been in existence in America for well over 100 years. The Westminster Kennel Club dog show, held in New York City every year in early February, is the second oldest annual sporting event in the country, with only the Kentucky Derby having greater longevity.

If you are new to the show ring, attend a few local shows without your dog to see what the game is about. If you are competitive, have the time and

Ch. Bushaway Remy Lefox and Ch. Lefox Goodtime Steel Magnolia make a statement.

If you feel that your Frenchie is of show quality and he is well trained, enter him in an AKC-licensed dog show.

money to compete, and of course, have a good dog, this may be the sport and hobby for you.

Contact your local all-breed club and find out if they offer conformation classes where you can learn how to handle your dog in the ring. Start attending these classes on a regular basis. One class does not an expert make! Your all-breed club will hold one or two matches a year, so you should plan to attend these matches. Match shows are run like a dog show, but they are casual and a good place for the beginner to learn. You will not receive any points toward a championship, but you will find out how a dog show is run and learn what will be expected of you and your dog. Entry fees are minimal. This is also a good opportunity to meet the people in the breed.

When you think you are ready—your dog can walk on a lead and you feel a tiny bit of confidence—enter an AKC-licensed dog show.

Remember that participating successfully in dog shows requires patience, time, money, skill, and talent. It is the only sport where the amateur and the professional compete on an equal footing. The average dog show competitor remains active for only three to four years. Personal commitments such as children, work, and other hobbies can be a problem to those who want to compete every weekend. More often, the competitor who does not win enough will find his interest in the sport waning. A poorly groomed dog, a poorly bred dog, a dog that does not like to show, and a handler who will not take the time to learn how to handle well are all deterrents to staying with the sport of dog showing.

It is always a pleasure to see a good Frenchie in the ring. The French Bulldog Club of America holds a national specialty show once a year. It is a prestigious show for the breed and it brings out the top competition throughout the country. Breeders show their stock, fanciers have the opportunity to see the upcoming winners in the breed, old friendships are renewed, and new acquaintances are made. In addition, seminars and meetings are held covering health, conformation, and possible problems for the breed. This is an event not to be missed for those who are active in breeding and showing the French Bulldog.

Participating in dog shows requires a lot of time, patience, and money. Before you commit to the sport, be sure that you can dedicate yourself to succeeding.

BREED CONCERNS

If you are considering buying your first French Bulldog, you must be aware that although he is a clown and a wonderful companion, the breed also has a fair number of health problems and requires more care than many other breeds. This breed is not considered an "easy keeper."

Before you decide to purchase a French Bulldog, be aware of the breed's health concerns. Although they are adorable pets and great companions, French Bulldogs are not free of certain health problems.

The French Bulldog is one of the brachycephalic breeds. These are the flat-faced, short-nosed dogs that also include, in addition to the Frenchie, the Bulldog, Pug, Boxer, and Boston Terrier. These breeds have abnormally small openings to the nostrils and relatively long palates. Dogs prefer to breathe through their nose, and for these breeds it becomes difficult for

them to breathe through the small nasal opening. Thus, the brachycelphalic breeds must increase their respiratory effort even when at rest.

Because of their breathing problems, Frenchies can be very susceptible to heat and cold, and caution must be taken, particularly in the summer months. Your Frenchie must never engage in strenuous activity in the heat and he must not be out in the cold any longer than necessary. Abnormal noise, such as snorting and snoring, are also very common with this breed. As a Frenchie owner, you will become very familiar with and used to these snorts and snores, even if your friends find it a bit humorous.

Frenchies have very short screw tails and can be prone to anal gland impaction. The dog has two anal glands (or sacs) that are located on either side of the rectum. These glands are the equivalent to the "scent" sacs in a skunk. In most breeds, it is relatively easy for the owner or groomer to express these sacs before giving the dog a bath. With the Frenchie, because of

Because of their breathing problems, be careful not to let your Frenchie engage in strenuous activity in the heat or stay out in the cold weather for an extended period of time.

the screw tail, it can be quite difficult for an amateur to express the glands. When you take your dog in for his yearly physical, you should have the veterinarian check the anal glands. In the meantime, if you should see your dog "scooting" along the ground repeatedly, it can be an indication that there is a problem. He should be taken to the veterinarian to be examined to see if the glands need to be cleaned. If this is a problem that is not taken care of, surgery will eventually be necessary to remove the glands.

Premature degeneration of the invertebrate discs can be a problem in the breed. Symptoms are a protruding or stiff neck, lameness in either front or rear legs, and loss of bladder control. You must see your veterinarian if the situation arises, and treatment will probably consist of either inflammatory drugs or surgery.

Uterine problems can occur in unspayed females, as well as pyometra and metritis. Natural births in the breed are uncommon due to the large head, large shoulders, and small pelvis, and a cesarean section will almost always be called for.

Juvenile cataracts can also be a problem. This is an inherited disorder and you should ask your breeder if she has had this problem in her line.

To prevent health complications, take your Frenchie to the vet for his routine checkups.

Skin allergies may occur in the breed. Allergies in dogs, just like allergies in humans, can be caused by pollen, dust, foods, and many other things in the environment. If possible, you should try to determine just what your dog is allergic to and then keep him away from whatever is causing his itchiness. If you are unable to locate the problem, and this can often be the case, you should take your dog to the veterinarian and see what course of action he suggests. Skin problems may often be difficult to clear up in any breed and sometimes all you can expect is to be able to give your animal some temporary relief, either through balms, medication, or bathing. Occasionally, your dog will only be affected at certain times of the year, as are humans who are allergic to ragweed and pollen.

Opposite: It's a good idea to become familiar with the French Bulldog breed and its special health concerns before acquiring one.

Cancer diagnosis is possible in any breed of dog and French Bulldogs are no exception. As in humans, there is not always a cure, and early detection is the best form of prevention. Each time you groom your dog, check him for any lumps or bumps that you have not noticed before. Fast-growing lumps are cause for concern, particularly when found around the mammary glands. Any lump that you do not like the look of or that is growing rapidly should be checked by your veterinarian.

For health problems, you must have a good veterinarian who is familiar with the breed and familiar with your dog.

Steve Eltinger wrote, "Lest the reader begin to feel that Frenchies are riddled with defects, it should be pointed out that all breeds have special problems...It is good to put each breed in perspective, by being aware of the problems that do not exist, as well as being prepared to deal with those that do."

Allergies can be caused by pollen, dust, food, and many other environmental components. If it's possible, keep your dog away from whatever is irritating his skin.

YOUR HEALTHY FRENCH BULLDOG

Dogs, like all other animals, are capable of contracting problems and diseases that, in most cases, are easily avoided by sound husbandry—meaning well-bred and well-cared-for animals are less prone to developing diseases and problems than are carelessly bred and neglected animals. Your knowledge of how to avoid problems is far more valuable than all of the books and advice on how to cure them. Respectively, the only person you should listen to about treatment is your vet. Veterinarians don't have all the answers, but at least they are trained to analyze and treat illnesses, and are aware of the full implications of treatments. This does not mean a few old remedies aren't good standbys when all else fails, but in most cases modern science provides the best treatments for disease.

Opposite: Although there are some faults that have a pregenetic disposition, most of these problems are not life threatening or debilitating.

PHYSICAL EXAMS

Your puppy should receive regular physical examinations or check-ups. These come in two forms. One is obviously performed by your vet, and the other is a day-to-day procedure that should be done by you. Apart from the fact the exam will highlight any problem at an early stage, it is an excellent way of socializing the pup to being handled.

To do the physical exam yourself, start at the head and work your way around the body. You are looking for any sign of lesions, or any indication of parasites on the pup. The most common parasites are fleas and ticks.

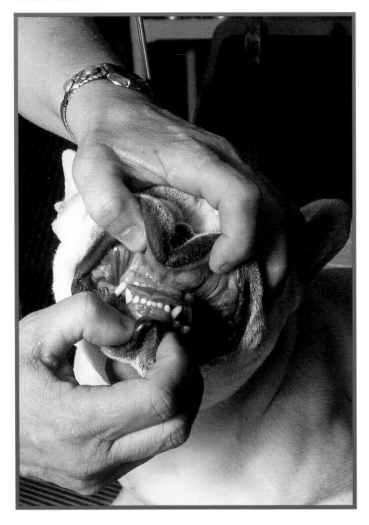

Your veterinarian should perform a thorough oral exam at every checkup to ensure your Frenchie's dental health.

HEALTHY TEETH AND GUMS

Chewing is instinctual. Puppies chew so that their teeth and jaws grow strong and healthy as they develop. As the permanent teeth begin to emerge, it is painful and annoying to the puppy, and puppy owners must recognize that their new charges need something safe upon which to chew. Unfortunately, once the puppy's permanent teeth have emerged and settled solidly into the jaw, the chewing instinct does not fade. Adult dogs instinctively need to clean their teeth, massage their gums, and exercise their jaws through chewing.

It is necessary for your dog to have clean teeth. You should take your dog to the veterinarian at least once a year to have his teeth cleaned and to have his mouth examined for any sign of oral disease. Although dogs do not get cavities in the same way humans do, dogs'

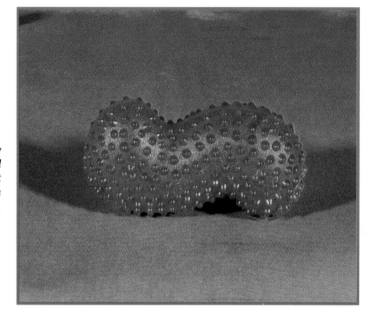

The Hercules™ by Nylabone® has raised dental tips that help fight plaque on your French Bulldog's teeth and gums.

teeth accumulate tartar, and more quickly than humans do! Veterinarians recommend brushing your dog's teeth daily. But who can find time to brush their dog's teeth daily? The accumulation of tartar and plaque on our dog's teeth when not removed can cause irritation and eventually erode the enamel and finally destroy the teeth. Advanced cases, while destroying the teeth, bring on gingivitis and periodontitis, two very serious conditions that can affect the dog's internal organs as well...to say nothing about bad breath!

Since everyone can't brush their dog's teeth daily or get to the veterinarian often enough for him to scale

Raised dental tips on the surface of every Plaque Attacker™ help to combat plaque and tartar.

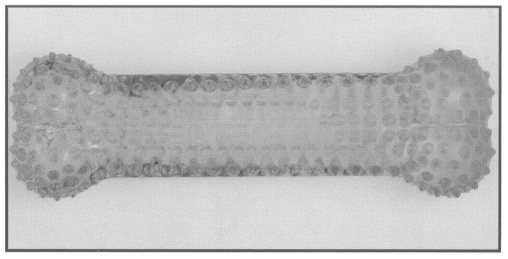

the dog's teeth, providing the dog with something safe to chew on will help maintain oral hygeine. Chew devices from Nylabone® keep dogs' teeth clean, but they also provide an excellent resource for entertainment and relief of doggie tensions. Nylabone® products give your dog something to do for an hour or two every day and during that hour or two, your dog will be taking an active part in keeping his teeth and gums healthy…without even realizing it! That's invaluable to your dog, and valuable to you!

Nylabone® provides fun bones, challenging bones, and *safe* bones. It is an owner's responsibility to recognize safe chew toys from dangerous ones. Your dog will chew and devour anything you give him. Dogs must not be permitted to chew on items that they can break. Pieces of broken objects can do internal damage to a dog, besides ripping the dog's mouth. Cheap plastic or rubber toys can cause stoppage in the intestines; such stoppages are operable only if caught immediately.

The most obvious choices, in this case, may be the worst choice. Natural beef bones were not designed for chewing and cannot take too much pressure from the sides. Due to the abrasive nature of these bones, they should be offered most sparingly. Knuckle bones, though once very popular for dogs, can be easily

Nylabone® is the only plastic dog bone made of 100 percent virgin nylon, specially processed to create a tough, durable, completely safe bone.

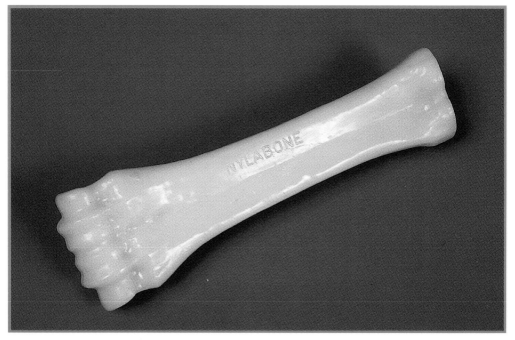

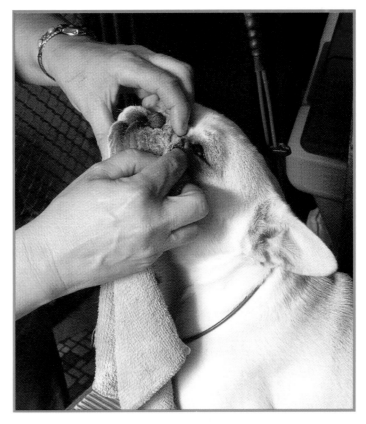

Routine grooming can help control parasite infestation. Examine your Frenchie's coat regularly for skin problems.

chewed up and eaten by dogs. At the very least, digestion is interrupted; at worst, the dog can choke or suffer from intestinal blockage.

When a dog chews hard on a Nylabone®, little bristle-like projections appear on the surface of the bone. These help to clean the dog's teeth and add to the gum-massaging. Given the chemistry of the nylon, the bristle can pass through the dog's intestinal tract without effect. Since nylon is inert, no microorganism can grow on it, and it can be washed in soap and water or sterilized in boiling water or in an autoclave.

For the sake of your dog, his teeth and your own peace of mind, provide your dog with Nylabones®. They have 100 variations from which to choose.

FIGHTING FLEAS

Fleas are very mobile and may be red, black, or brown in color. The adults suck the blood of the host, while the larvae feed on the feces of the adults, which is rich in blood. Flea "dirt" may be seen on the pup as very tiny clusters of blackish specks that look like freshly ground pepper. The eggs of fleas may be laid on the puppy, though they are more commonly laid off the host in a favorable place, such as the bedding. They normally hatch in 4 to 21 days, depending on the temperature, but they can survive for up to 18 months if temperature conditions are not favorable. The larvae are maggot-like and molt a couple of times before forming pupae, which can survive long periods until the temperature, or the vibration of a nearby host, causes them to emerge and jump on a host.

There are a number of effective treatments available, and you should discuss them with your veterinarian, then follow all instructions for the one you choose. Any treatment will involve a product for your puppy or dog and one for the environment, and will require diligence on your part to treat all areas and thoroughly clean your home and yard until the infestation is eradicated.

THE TROUBLE WITH TICKS

Ticks are arthropods of the spider family, which means they have eight legs (though the larvae have six). They bury their headparts into the host and gorge on its blood. They are easily seen as small grain-like creatures sticking out from the skin. They are often picked up when dogs play in fields, but may also arrive in your yard via wild animals—even birds—or stray cats and dogs. Some ticks are species-specific, others are more adaptable and will host on many species.

The cat flea is the most common flea of dogs. It starts feeding soon after it makes contact with the dog.

The deer tick is the most common carrier of Lyme disease. Photo courtesy of Virbac Laboratories, Inc., Fort Worth, Texas.

The most troublesome type of tick is the deer tick, which spreads the deadly Lyme disease that can cripple a dog (or a person). Deer ticks are tiny and very hard to detect. Often, by the time they're big enough to notice, they've been feeding on the dog for a few days—long enough to do their damage. Lyme disease was named for the area of the United States in which it was first detected—Lyme, Connecticut—but has now been diagnosed in almost all parts of the U.S. Your veterinarian can advise you of the danger to your dog(s) in your area, and may suggest your dog be vaccinated for Lyme. Always go over your dog with a fine-toothed flea comb when you come in from walking through any area that may harbor deer ticks, and if your dog is acting unusually sluggish or sore, seek veterinary advice.

Attempts to pull a tick free will invariably leave the headpart in the pup, where it will die and cause an infected wound or abscess. The best way to remove ticks is to dab a strong saline solution, iodine, or alcohol on them. This will numb them, causing them to loosen their hold, at which time they can be removed with forceps. The wound can then be cleaned and covered with an antiseptic ointment. If ticks are common in your area, consult with your vet for a suitable pesticide to be used in kennels, on bedding, and on the puppy or dog.

INSECTS AND OTHER OUTDOOR DANGERS

There are many biting insects, such as mosquitoes, that can cause discomfort to a puppy. Many diseases are transmitted by the males of these species.

A pup can easily get a grass seed or thorn lodged between his pads or in the folds of his ears. These may go unnoticed until an abscess forms.

This is where your daily check of the puppy or dog will do a world of good. If your puppy has been playing in long grass or places where there may be thorns, pine needles, wild animals, or parasites, the check-up is a wise precaution.

Your French Bulldog may encounter fleas or ticks when playing outside. Be sure to check his coat for any parasites.

SKIN DISORDERS

Apart from problems associated with lesions created by biting pests, a puppy may fall foul to a number of other skin disorders. Examples are ringworm, mange, and eczema. Ringworm is not caused by a worm, but is a fungal infection. It manifests itself as a sore-looking bald circle. If your puppy should have any form of bald patches, let your veterinarian check him over; a microscopic examination can confirm the condition. Many old remedies for ringworm exist, such as iodine, carbolic acid, formalin, and other tinctures, but modern drugs are superior.

Fungal infections can be very difficult to treat, and even more difficult to eradicate, because of the spores. These can withstand most treatments, other than burning, which is the best thing to do with bedding once the condition has been confirmed.

Mange is a general term that can be applied to many skin conditions where the hair falls out and a flaky crust develops and falls away.

Often, dogs will scratch themselves, and this invariably is worse than the original condition, for it opens lesions that are then subject to viral, fungal, or parasitic attack. The cause of the problem can be various species of mites. These either live on skin debris and the hair follicles, which they destroy, or they bury themselves just beneath the skin and feed on the tissue. Applying general remedies from pet stores is not recommended because it is essential to identify the type of mange before a specific treatment is effective.

Eczema is another non-specific term applied to many skin disorders. The condition can be brought about in many ways. Sunburn, chemicals, allergies to foods, drugs, pollens, and even stress can all produce a deterioration of the skin and coat. Given the range of causal factors, treatment can be difficult because the problem is one of identification. It is a case of taking each possibility at a time and trying to correctly diagnose the matter. If the cause is of a dietary nature then you must remove one item at a time in order to find out if the dog is allergic to a given food. It could, of course, be the lack of a nutrient that is the problem, so if the condition persists, you should consult your veterinarian.

INTERNAL DISORDERS

It cannot be overstressed that it is very foolish to attempt to diagnose an internal disorder without the advice of a veterinarian. Take a relatively common problem such as diarrhea. It might be caused by nothing more serious than the puppy hogging a lot of food or eating something that it has never previously eaten. Conversely, it could be the first indication of a potentially fatal disease. It's up to your veterinarian to make the correct diagnosis.

The following symptoms, especially if they accompany each other or are progressively added to earlier symptoms, mean you should visit the veterinarian right away:

Continual vomiting. All dogs vomit from time to time and this is not necessarily a sign of illness. They will eat grass to induce vomiting. It is a natural cleansing process common to many carnivores. However, continued vomiting is a clear sign of a problem. It may be a blockage in the pup's intestinal tract, it may be induced by worms, or it could be due to any number of diseases.

Diarrhea. This, too, may be nothing more than a temporary condition due to many factors. Even a change of home can induce diarrhea, because this often stresses the pup, and invariably there is some change in the diet. If it persists more than 48 hours then something is amiss. If blood is seen in the feces, waste no time at all in taking the dog to the vet.

Running eyes and/or nose. A pup might have a chill and this will cause the eyes and nose to weep. Again, this should quickly clear up if the puppy is placed in a warm environment and away from any drafts. If it does not, and especially if a mucous discharge is seen, then the pup has an illness that must be diagnosed.

Coughing. Prolonged coughing is a sign of a problem, usually of a respiratory nature.

Wheezing. If the pup has difficulty breathing and makes a wheezing sound when breathing, then something is wrong.

Cries when attempting to defecate or urinate. This might only be a minor problem due to the hard state of the feces, but it could be more serious, especially if the pup cries when urinating.

Cries when touched. Obviously, if you do not handle a puppy with care he might yelp. However, if he cries even when lifted gently, then he has an internal problem that becomes apparent when pressure is applied to a given area of the body. Clearly, this must be diagnosed.

Refuses food. Generally, puppies and dogs are greedy creatures when it comes to feeding time. Some might be more fussy, but none should refuse more than one meal. If they go for a number of hours without showing any interest in their food, then something is not as it should be.

General listlessness. All puppies have their off days when they do not seem their usual cheeky, mischievous selves. If this condition persists for more than two days then there is little doubt of a problem. They may not show any of the signs listed, other than perhaps a reduced interest in their food. There are many diseases that can develop internally without displaying obvious clinical signs. Blood, fecal, and other tests are needed in order to identify the disorder before it reaches an advanced state that may not be treatable.

WORMS

There are many species of worms, and a number of these live in the tissues of dogs and most other animals. Many create no problem at all, so you are not even aware they exist. Others can be tolerated in small levels, but become a major problem if they number more than a few. The most common types seen in dogs are roundworms and tapeworms. While roundworms are the greater problem, tapeworms require an intermediate host so are more easily eradicated.

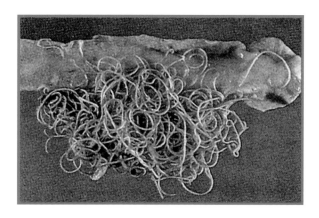

Roundworms are spaghetti-like worms that cause a pot-bellied appearance and dull coat, along with more severe symptoms, such as diarrhea and vomiting. Photo courtesy of Merck AgVet.

Roundworms of the species *Toxocara canis* infest the dog. They may grow to a length of 8 inches (20 cm) and look like strings of spaghetti. The worms feed on the digesting food in the pup's intestines. In chronic cases the puppy will become pot-bellied, have diarrhea, and will vomit. Eventually, he will stop eating, having passed through the stage when he always seems hungry. The worms lay eggs in the puppy and these pass out in his feces. They are then either ingested by the pup, or they are eaten by mice, rats, or beetles. These may then be eaten by the puppy and the life cycle is complete.

Larval worms can migrate to the womb of a pregnant bitch, or to her mammary glands, and this is how they pass to the puppy. The pregnant bitch can be wormed, which will help. The pups can, and should,

Whipworms are hard to find unless you strain your dog's feces, and this is best left to a veterinarian. Pictured here are adult whipworms.

be wormed when they are about two weeks old. Repeat worming every 10 to 14 days and the parasites should be removed. Worms can be extremely dangerous to young puppies, so you should be sure the pup is wormed as a matter of routine.

Tapeworms can be seen as tiny rice-like eggs sticking to the puppy's or dog's anus. They are less destructive, but still undesirable. The eggs are eaten by mice, fleas, rabbits, and other animals that serve as intermediate hosts. They develop into a larval stage and the host must be eaten by the dog in order to complete the chain. Your vet will supply a suitable remedy if tapeworms are seen or suspected. There are other worms, such as hookworms and whipworms, that are also blood suckers. They will make a pup anemic, and blood might be seen in the feces, which can be examined by the vet to confirm their presence. Cleanliness in all matters is the best preventative measure for all worms.

Heartworm infestation in dogs is passed by mosquitoes but can be prevented by a monthly (or daily) treatment that is given orally. Talk to your vet about the risk of heartworm in your area.

BLOAT (GASTRIC DILATATION)

This condition has proved fatal in many dogs, especially large and deep-chested breeds, such as the Weimaraner and the Great Dane. However, any dog can get bloat. It is caused by swallowing air during exercise, food/water gulping or another strenuous task. As many believe, it is not the result of flatulence. The stomach of an affected dog twists, disallowing food and blood flow and resulting in harmful toxins being released into the bloodstream. Death can easily follow if the condition goes undetected.

The best preventative measure is not to feed large meals or exercise your puppy or dog immediately after he has eaten. Veterinarians recommend feeding three smaller meals per day in an elevated feeding rack, adding water to dry food to prevent gulping, and not offering water during mealtimes.

VACCINATIONS

Every puppy, purebred or mixed breed, should be vaccinated against the major canine diseases. These are distemper, leptospirosis, hepatitis, and canine parvovirus. Your puppy may have received a temporary vaccination against distemper before you purchased him, but be sure to ask the breeder to be sure.

The age at which vaccinations are given can vary, but will usually be when the pup is 8 to 12 weeks old. By this time any protection given to the pup by antibodies received from his mother via her initial milk feeds will be losing their strength.

Rely on your veterinarian for the most effectual vaccination schedule for your French Bulldog puppy.

The puppy's immune system works on the basis that the white blood cells engulf and render harmless

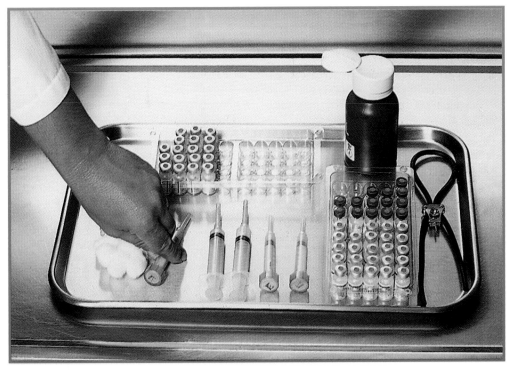

attacking bacteria. However, they must first recognize a potential enemy.

Vaccines are either dead bacteria or they are live, but in very small doses. Either type prompts the pup's defense system to attack them. When a large attack then comes (if it does), the immune system recognizes it and massive numbers of lymphocytes (white blood corpuscles) are mobilized to counter the attack. However, the ability of the cells to recognize these dangerous viruses can diminish over a period of time. It is therefore useful to provide annual reminders about the nature of the enemy. This is done by means of booster injections that keep the immune system on its alert. Immunization is not 100-percent guaranteed to be successful, but is very close. Certainly it is better than giving the puppy no protection.

Dogs are subject to other viral attacks, and if these are of a high-risk factor in your area, then your vet will suggest you have the puppy vaccinated against these as well.

Your puppy or dog should also be vaccinated against the deadly rabies virus. In fact, in many places it is illegal for your dog not to be vaccinated. This is to protect your dog, your family, and the rest of the animal population from this deadly virus that infects the nervous system and causes dementia and death.

ACCIDENTS

All puppies will get their share of bumps and bruises due to the rather energetic way they play. These will usually heal themselves over a few days. Small cuts should be bathed with a suitable disinfectant and then smeared with an antiseptic ointment. If a cut looks more serious, then stem the flow of blood with a towel or makeshift tourniquet and rush the pup to the veterinarian. Never apply so much pressure to the wound that it might restrict the flow of blood to the limb.

In the case of burns you should apply cold water or an ice pack to the surface. If the burn was due to a chemical, then this must be washed away with copious amounts of water. Apply petroleum jelly, or any vegetable oil, to the burn. Trim away the hair if need be. Wrap the dog in a blanket and rush him to the vet. The pup may go into shock, depending on the severity of the burn, and this will result in a lowered blood pressure, which is dangerous and the reason the pup must receive immediate veterinary attention.

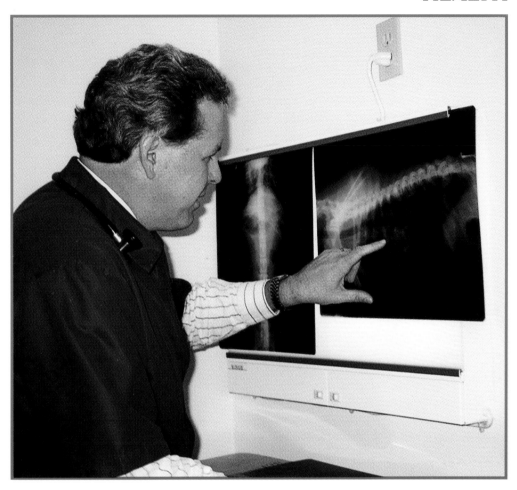

It is a good idea to x-ray the chest and abdomen on any dog hit by a car.

If a broken limb is suspected then try to keep the animal as still as possible. Wrap your pup or dog in a blanket to restrict movement and get him to the veterinarian as soon as possible. Do not move the dog's head so it is tilting backward, as this might result in blood entering the lungs.

Do not let your pup jump up and down from heights, as this can cause considerable shock to the joints. Like all youngsters, puppies do not know when enough is enough, so you must do all their thinking for them.

Provided you apply strict hygiene to all aspects of raising your puppy, and you make daily checks on his physical state, you have done as much as you can to safeguard him during his most vulnerable period. Routine visits to your veterinarian are also recommended, especially while the puppy is under one year of age. The vet may notice something that did not seem important to you.

CONGENITAL AND ACQUIRED DISORDERS

by Judy Iby, RVT

Veterinarians and breeders now recognize that many of the disease processes and faults in dogs, as well as in human beings, have a genetic predisposition. These faults are found not only in the purebred dog but in the mixed breed as well. Likely these diseases have been present for decades but more recently are being identified and attributed to inheritance. Fortunately many of these problems are not life threatening or even debilitating. Many of these disorders have a low incidence. It is true that some breeds and some bloodlines within a breed have a higher frequency than others. It is always wise to discuss this subject with breeders of your breed.

Presently very few of the hundreds of disorders can be identified through genetic testing. Hopefully with today's technology and the desire to improve our breeding stock, genetic testing will become more readily available. In the meantime the reputable breeder does the recommended testing for his breed. The American Kennel Club is encouraging OFA (Orthopedic Foundation for Animals) hip and elbow certification and CERF (Canine Eye Registration Foundation) certifications and is listing them on AKC registrations and pedigrees. This is a step forward for the AKC in encouraging better breeding. They also founded a Canine Health Foundation to aid in the research of diseases in the purebred dog.

BONES AND JOINTS

Hip Dysplasia

Canine hip dysplasia has been confirmed in 79 breeds. It is the malformation of the hip joint's ball and socket, with clinical signs from none to severe hip lameness. It may appear as early as five months. The incidence is

Opposite: You want your dog to be as healthy as possible. Scheduled visits to the vet can help detect various problems or complications.

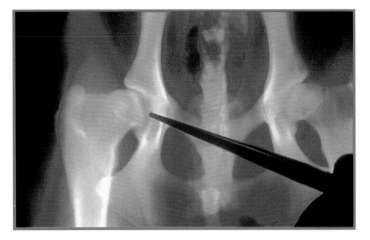

Radiograph of a dog with hip dysplasia. Note the flattened femoral head at the marker. Photo courtesy of Toronto Academy of Veterinary Medicine, Toronto, Canada.

reduced within a bloodline by breeding normal to normal, generation after generation. Upon submitting normal pelvic radiographs, the OFA will issue a certification number.

Elbow Dysplasia

Elbow dysplasia results from abnormal development of the ulna, one of the bones of the upper arm. During bone growth, a small area of bone (the anconeal process) fails to fuse with the rest of the bone. This results in an unstable elbow joint and lameness, which is aggravated by exercise. OFA certifies free of this disorder.

Patellar Luxation

This condition can be medial or lateral. Breeders call patellar luxations "slips" for "slipped kneecaps." OFA offers a registry for this disorder. Patellar luxations may or may not cause problems.

Intervertebral Disk Disease (IVD)

IVD is a condition in which a disk(s), the cushion between each vertebrae of the spine, tears and the gel-like material leaks out and presses on the spinal cord. The degeneration is progressive, starting as early as two to nine months, but usually the neurological symptoms are not apparent until three to six years of age. Symptoms include pain, paresis (weariness), incoordination, and paralysis. IVD is a medical emergency. If you are unable to get professional care immediately, then confine your dog to a crate or small area until he can be seen.

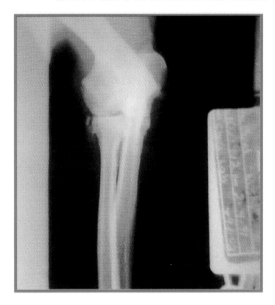

Fragmented coronoid process of the elbow, a manifestation of elbow dysplasia. Photo courtesy of Jack Henry.

Spondylitis

Usually seen in middle to old-age dogs and potentially quite serious in the latter, spondylitis is inflammation of the vertebral joints and degeneration of intervertebral disks resulting in bony spur-like outgrowths that may fuse.

CARDIOVASCULAR AND LYMPHATIC SYSTEMS

Dilated Cardiomyopathy

Prevalent in several breeds, this is a disease in which the heart muscle is damaged or destroyed to the point that it cannot pump blood properly through the body resulting in signs of heart failure. Diagnosis is confirmed by cardiac ultrasound.

Lymphosarcoma

This condition can occur in young dogs but usually appears in dogs over the age of five years. Symptoms include fever, weight loss, anorexia, painless enlargement of the lymph nodes, and nonspecific signs of illness. It is the most common type of cancer found in dogs. Chemotherapy treatment will prolong the dog's life but will not cure the disease at this time.

BLOOD

Von Willebrand's Disease

VWD has been confirmed in over 50 breeds and is

a manageable disease. It is characterized by moderate to severe bleeding, corrected by blood transfusions from normal dogs and frequently seen with hypothyroidism. When levels are low, a pre-surgical blood transfusion may be necessary. Many breeders screen their breeding stock for vWD.

Immune-Mediated Blood Disease
Immune-mediated diseases affect the red blood cells and platelets. They are called autoimmune hemolytic anemia or immune-mediated anemia when red blood cells are affected, and autoimmune thrombocytopenic purpura, idiopathic thrombocytopenic purpura, and immune-mediated thrombocytopenia when platelets are involved. The disease may appear acutely. Symptoms include jaundice (yellow color) of the gums and eyes and dark brown or dark red urine. Symptoms of platelet disease include pinpoint bruises or hemorrhages in the skin, gums and eye membranes; nosebleeds; bleeding from the GI tract or into the urine. Any of these symptoms constitutes an emergency!

DIGESTIVE SYSTEM AND ORAL CAVITY

Colitis
This disorder has no known cause and appears with some frequency in certain breeds. It is characterized by an intermittent bloody stool, with or without diarrhea.

Chronic Hepatitis
This is the result of liver failure occuring at relatively young ages. In many cases clinical signs are apparent for less than two weeks. They include anorexia, lethargy, vomiting, depression, diarrhea, trembling or shaking, excess thirst and urination, weight loss, and dark bloody stool. Early diagnosis and treatment promise the best chance for survival.

Copper Toxicity
Copper toxicity occurs when excessive copper is concentrated in the liver. In 1995 there was a breakthrough when the DNA marker was identified in one of the afflicted breeds. Therefore carriers will be identified in the future.

ENDOCRINE SYSTEM

Hypothyroidism

Over 50 breeds have been diagnosed with hypothyroidism. It is the number-one endocrine disorder in the dog and is the result of an underactive thyroid gland. Conscientious breeders are screening their dogs if the disease is common to their breed or bloodline. The critical years for the decline of thyroid function are usually between three and eight, although it can appear at an older age. A simple blood test can diagnose or rule out this disorder. It is easily and inexpensively treated by giving thyroid replacement therapy daily. Untreated hypothyroidism can be devastating to your dog.

Addison's Disease

Primary adrenal insufficiency is caused by damage to the adrenal cortex, and secondary adrenocortical insufficiency is the result of insufficient production of the hormone ACTH by the pituitary gland. Symptoms may include depression, anorexia, a weak femoral pulse, vomiting or diarrhea, weakness, dehydration, and occasionally bradycardia.

Cushing's Disease

Hyperadrenocorticism is the over-production of steroid hormone. Dogs on steroid therapy may show Cushing-like symptoms. Some of the symptoms are excess thirst and urination, hair loss, and an enlarged, pendulous, or flaccid abdomen.

EYES

Cataracts

Breeders should screen their breeding stock for this disorder. A cataract is defined as any opacity of the lens or its capsule. It may progress and produce blindness or it may remain small and cause no clinical impairment of vision. Unfortunately some inherited cataracts appear later in life after the dog has already been bred.

Lens Luxation

This condition results when the lens of the eye is not in normal position, and may result in secondary glaucoma.

Glaucoma

Primary glaucoma is caused by increased intraocular pressure due to inadequate aqueous drainage and is not associated with other intraocular diseases. It may initially be in one eye. Secondary glaucoma is caused by increased intraocular pressure brought on by another ocular disease, tumor, or inflammation.

Keratoconjunctivitis Sicca

"Dry eye" (the decrease in production of tears) may be the result of a congenital or inherited deficiency of the aqueous layer, a lack of the proper nervous stimulation of the tearing system, a traumatic incident, or drugs, including topical anesthetics (such as

An immature cataract is evident in this dilated pupil. The central white area and cloudy areas at 4:00, 6:00 and 8:00 represent the cataract. Photo courtesy of Dr. Kerry L. Ketring.

atropine, and antibiotics containing sulfadiazine, phenazopyridine or salicyla-sulfapyridine). There seems to be an increased incidence of "dry eye" after "cherry eye" removal.

Progressive Retinal Atrophy (PRA)

This is the progressive loss of vision, first at night, followed by total blindness. It is inherited in many breeds.

Distichiasis

Distichiasis results from extra rows of eyelashes growing out of the meibomian gland ducts. This condition may cause tearing, but tearing may be the result of some other problem that needs to be investigated.

Entropion
Entropion is the inward rolling of the eyelid, usually lower lid, which can cause inflammation and may need surgical correction.

Ectropion
Ectropion is the outward rolling of the eyelid, usually lower lid, and may need surgical correction.

Hypertrophy of the Nictitans Gland
"Cherry eye" is the increase in size of the gland resulting in eversion of the third eyelid and is usually bilateral. Onset frequently occurs during stressful periods such as teething.

NEUROMUSCULAR SYSTEM

Epilepsy
Epilepsy is a disorder in which the electrical brain activity "short circuits," resulting in a seizure. Numerous breeds and mixed breeds are subject to idiopathic epilepsy (no explainable reason). Seizures usually begin between six months and five years of age. Don't panic. Your primary concern should be to keep your dog from hurting himself by falling down the stairs or falling off furniture and/or banging his head. Dogs don't swallow their tongues. If the seizure lasts longer than ten minutes, you should contact your veterinarian. Seizures can be caused by many conditions, such as poisoning and birth injuries, brain infections, trauma or tumors, liver disease, distemper, and low blood sugar or calcium. There are all types of seizures from generalized (the dog will be shaking and paddling/kicking his feet) to standing and staring out in space, etc.

UROGENITAL

Cryptorchidism
This is a condition in which either one or both of the testes fail to descend into the scrotum. There should not be a problem if the dog is neutered early, before two to three years of age. Otherwise, the undescended testicle could turn cancerous.

PET OWNERS & BLOOD PRESSURE

Over the past few years, several scientific studies have documented many health benefits of having pets in our lives. At the State University of New York at Buffalo, for example, Dr. Karen Allen and her colleagues have focused on how physical reactions to psychological stress are influenced by the presence of pets. One such study compared the effect of pets with that of a person's close friend and reported pets to be dramatically better than friends at providing unconditional support. Blood pressure was monitored throughout the study, and, on average, the blood pressure of people under stress who were *with* their pets was 112/75, as compared to 140/95 when they were with the self-selected friends. Heart rate differences were also significantly lower when participants were with their pets. A follow-up study included married couples and looked at the stress-reducing effect of pets versus *spouses*, and found, once again, that pets were dramatically more successful than other people in reducing cardiovascular reactions to stress. An interesting discovery made in this study was that when the spouse and pet were *both* present, heart rate and blood pressure came down dramatically.

Other work by the same researchers has looked at the role of pets in moderating age-related increases in blood pressure. In a study that followed 100 women (half in their 20s and half in their 70s) over six months, it was found that elderly women with few social contacts and *no* pets had blood pressures that were significantly higher (averages of 145/95 compared to 120/80) than elderly women with their beloved pets but few *human* contacts. In other words, elderly women with pets, but no friends, had blood pressures that closely reflected the blood pressures of young women.

This series of studies demonstrates that pets can play an important role in how we handle everyday stress, and shows that biological aging cannot be fully understood without a consideration of the social factors in our lives.

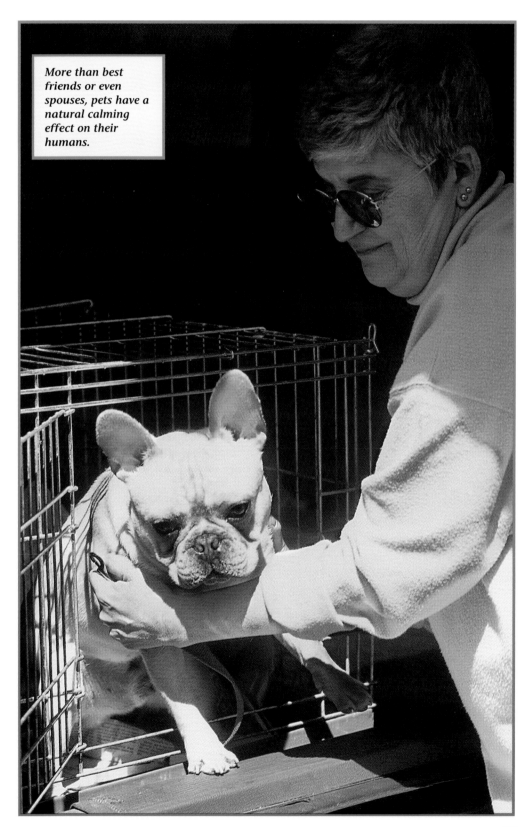

More than best friends or even spouses, pets have a natural calming effect on their humans.

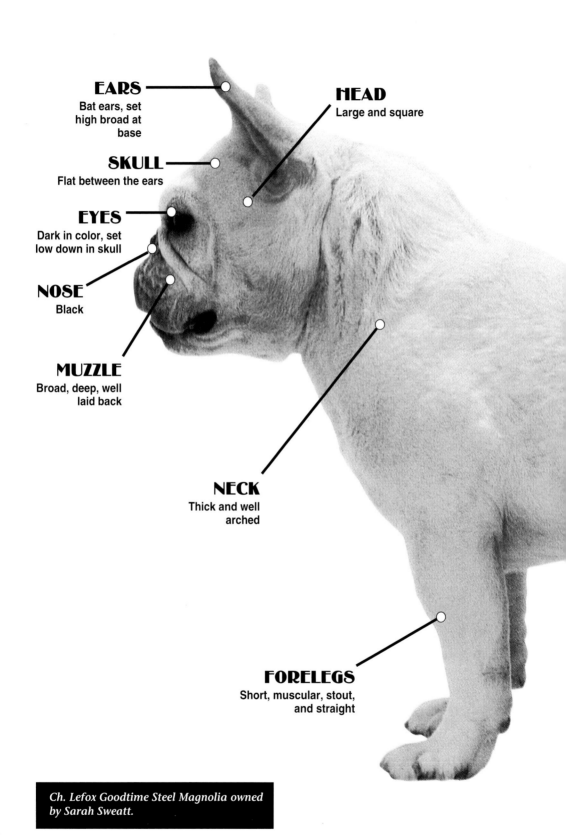

EARS
Bat ears, set
high broad at
base

HEAD
Large and square

SKULL
Flat between the ears

EYES
Dark in color, set
low down in skull

NOSE
Black

MUZZLE
Broad, deep, well
laid back

NECK
Thick and well
arched

FORELEGS
Short, muscular, stout,
and straight

*Ch. Lefox Goodtime Steel Magnolia owned
by Sarah Sweatt.*